WORK SHARING
CASE STUDIES

Maureen E. McCarthy
Gail S. Rosenberg
With assistance from Gary Lefkowitz

The material in this project was prepared under Contract No. 21-11-79-17 from the Employment and Training Administration, U.S. Department of Labor, under the authority of Title III, part B, of the Comprehensive Employment and Training Act of 1973. Researchers undertaking such projects under Government sponsorship are encouraged to express freely their professional judgment. Therefore, points of view or opinions stated in this document do not necessarily represent the official position or policy of the Department of Labor.

The W.E. Upjohn Institute for Employment Research

Library of Congress Cataloging in Publication Data

McCarthy, Maureen E.
  Work sharing case studies.

  Bibliography: p.
  1. Work sharing—United States—Case studies.
  I. Rosenberg, Gail S.   II. Lefkowitz, Gary.
  III. W.E. Upjohn Institute for Employment Research.
  IV. Title.
  HD5110.6.U6M35   331.25'72   81-15943
  ISBN 0-911558-87-X   AACR2
  ISBN 0-911558-88-8 (pbk.)

THE INSTITUTE, a nonprofit research organization, was established on July 1, 1945. It is an activity of the W. E. Upjohn Unemployment Trustee Corporation, which was formed in 1932 to administer a fund set aside by the late Dr. W. E. Upjohn for the purpose of carrying on "research into the causes and effects of unemployment and measures for the alleviation of unemployment."

The Board of Trustees
of the
W. E. Upjohn
Unemployment Trustee Corporation

The Staff of the Institute

DEDICATIONS

To my family and friends—who share their work and their love.

M.E.M.

To my husband Michael and our children Jeremy and Rebecca who make work sharing a valued option at this time of my life.

G.S.R.

AUTHORS

Maureen E. McCarthy is an independent consultant based in Columbia, Maryland, working with clients in the public and private sector in the design and implementation of new work patterns. Her current research interest is the impact of new office technology on work effectiveness and the development of motivational work design.

Ms. McCarthy was formerly vice president of the National Council for Alternative Work Patterns. She served as a consultant to the U.S. Department of Labor on an exploratory survey of short-time compensation and to the American Association of Retired Persons on flexible retirement options. She also was an advisor to a Department of Energy project examining the impact of alternative work patterns on energy and transportation. Ms. McCarthy has published articles in *Aging and Work, Personnel Administration,* and *Industrial Engineering.*

Gail S. Rosenberg is president of the National Council for Alternative Work Patterns. She was a consultant to the Department of Labor study on short-time compensation and the American Association of Retired Persons on flexible retirement options. She is a member of the Task Force on Alternative Work Patterns of the Work in America Institute.

Ms. Rosenberg edited the *Alternative Work Schedule Directory* (1978), co-authored a study on phased retirement experiments for the Summer 1980 issue of *Aging and Work,* and is past editor and current contributor to the *NCAWP Newsletter.* Her article on supervisory part-time federal employees appeared in the *Washington Post* in February 1980.

Gary Lefkowitz is president of Lieb, Lefkowitz and Associates, Inc., a firm which specializes in developing human resources at the workplace. He is also an Adjunct Lecturer in Labor Relations and Work Improvement in the Harriman College graduate program of the State University of New York at Stony Brook.

ACKNOWLEDGEMENTS

A number of people provided information and support for this book. We are most indebted to our colleagues at the National Council for Alternative Work Patterns, Marion C. Long, who served as the project research coordinator, and Susan W. Post, the project administrator. Dr. Fred Best, whose extensive research on flexible life scheduling served as the springboard for our work, provided strong encouragement for us to undertake the project.

We are grateful to Dr. Burt Barnow, acting director, Office of Research and Development, Office of Policy Evaluation and Research, Employment and Training Administration, U.S. Department of Labor, for awarding a grant to the National Council for Alternative Work Patterns to study work sharing in American organizations. Our project officer, Dr. Tom Joyce, was accessible and knowledgeable, and made many helpful suggestions regarding content.

Our special thanks are extended to Dr. E. Earl Wright, director of the W.E. Upjohn Institute for Employment Research, for his direction and encouragement in preparing this publication. He has had the foresight to examine work sharing from a variety of approaches in the W.E. Upjohn Institute series.

Several people contributed their special resources. Dr. Stanley Cohen from the Office of Personnel Management advised us on research methodology. Dr. Erica King served as consultant on the survey design. Gwen Wooley, Dr. Barbara Crispin, Nancy Inui, Barbara Metcalf, and Randi Bobman assisted in the literature search and company identification process throughout the country. Susan Powell designed the questionnaire format and coordinated its production.

Those who generously gave technical advice and shared ideas on the survey instrument are: David Arnold, National Governors' Association; William Batt, U.S. Department of Labor; Dr. Robert Bednarzik, Bureau of Labor Statistics; Joseph Cahalan, Xerox Corporation; Patsy Fryman, Communications Workers of America; Jim Harvey, Varian Associates; Dr. Janice Hedges, Bureau of Labor Statistics; Gladys Henrikson, consultant; Nadeanne Herrell, American Telephone and Telegraph; Linda Ittner, staff, U.S. House of Representatives Subcommittee on Civil Service; Ronna Klingenberg, American Council on Life Insurance; Virginia Martin, consultant; Oscar Mueller, U.S. Department of the Interior; Dr. Stanley Nollen, Georgetown University; Joseph Perkins, Polaroid Corporation; Robert Rosenberg, California State Office of Research; Frank Schiff, Committee for Economic Development; Rita Williams, ALZA Corporation; Jacques Wimpheimer, American Velvet; John Zalusky, AFL-CIO; and Bernard Zwinak, American Federation of Government Employees.

Special recognition is due Sherrell Varner who provided invaluable comments on organization and presentation. We thank Dr. Constance Swank for making information available on her forthcoming publication and for her encouragement. And we want to thank Judy Brawer, our capable editor at the Upjohn Institute, for her thoroughness and good humor.

Above all, we want to give special thanks to the many executives, officers, and staff people from companies, agencies, unions, and legislative offices who provided us with the information that serves as the heart of this book.

While we take full responsibility for the content of the book, we are grateful to all these people for their contributions.

M.E.M.
G.S.R.

FOREWORD

Private sector employers have expressed a need for practical, concrete information to determine the viability of work sharing as a way of meeting the changing goals and objectives of the organization and its employees. *Work Sharing Case Studies* responds to that need by presenting 36 cases in which the various forms of work sharing have been adopted.

Work sharing approaches described in the case studies represent a broad range of organizations—from Fortune 500 companies to small, family-owned firms. They were designed to meet a variety of specific corporate needs: to avoid layoffs, adjust to skill shortages, prevent employee burnout, adapt to changes in the workforce, achieve production flexibility, and recruit and retain valued employees. The information should be of value to business, union, and government officials in understanding the legislative and public policy implications of work sharing.

Facts and observations as presented in this monograph are the sole responsibility of the authors. Their viewpoints do not necessarily represent positions of the W.E. Upjohn Institute for Employment Research.

E. Earl Wright
Director

Kalamazoo, MI
September 1981

CONTENTS

INTRODUCTION

Work sharing is broadly defined as reduced work hour approaches that have the effect of sharing the available work among a greater number of persons. Although work scheduling arrangements may be adopted for a variety of reasons, we classify all arrangements that have the potential to preserve jobs and/or to provide additional job opportunities as work sharing—even when these are not the intended or chief outcomes. This book describes a variety of work sharing arrangements implemented by organizations throughout the United States—programs as diverse as rotation layoff, job sharing, extended holiday and vacations, social service leaves, and phased retirement.

Our primary purpose is to provide private sector employers with the practical, concrete information they need and seek to determine the viability of various work sharing arrangements. The book demonstrates the wide variety of occupations, technologies, and industries in which work sharing has been effectively implemented.

Moreover, this information will assist union and government officials in understanding the legislative and public policy implications of different work sharing arrangements. Because all these groups are actively seeking flexible solutions to a changing work environment, we have included programs adopted for a wide variety of reasons and have given special attention to the ways programs have been adapted to meet the changing goals and objectives of organizations and their employees. In this sense then, the book is a starting point in promoting more serious dialogue about the conditions under which work sharing is successful and in stimulating more vigorous and systematic work sharing research.

To provide pragmatic information, we have adopted a case study format. In addition to the general descriptions of programs presented at the beginning of each chapter, some 36 programs are described in depth—from the circumstances leading to adoption, through details of compensation and administrative arrangements, to perceived and measured advantages and disadvantages. Most of the case studies are from the private profitmaking sector, which constitutes the major portion of U.S. employment. However, some public sector initiatives which stand out for their innovation are also described.[1] Of the organizations represented in the case studies, 14 are unionized and 22 are nonunionized. Table 1 describes the organizations by type of industry, sector, and size.[2] Table 2 illustrates the distribution by size of unionized and nonunionized organizations. The book emphasizes the factors employers consider as they decide whether to adopt, and then how to design, reduced work hour arrangements—and on the process of implementation itself. In some instances, the effects of the programs on employee participants and their families are examined.

General Findings

Types of Programs

Work sharing arrangements fall into three general categories—temporary reduction in work hours, permanent reduction in work hours, and flexible worklife options—as outlined below.

---

1. Areas in which work patterns traditionally have been less rigid—nonprofit organizations, educational institutions, and youth programs—were deliberately excluded.

2. Due to the research procedure, described on pages 12-14, our sample may not be representative of U.S. employers and no generalized inference can be made from the data.

Table 1 Organizations by Type of Industry, Sector, and Size

Size of organization by number of employees*	Type of organization		
	Service	Private Manufacturing	Public agencies
500 or fewer	0	4	3
501 - 3,500	2	8	0
3,501 - 10,000	2	1	2
10,001 or more	3	9	2
TOTALS	7	22	7

*In a few cases where we were dealing with a unit or division of a firm or public agency, or only with those employees eligible to participate in the designated program, we use another set of numbers, which is explained in the individual case studies. This table is designed to give some sense of the distribution of the case studies and is not intended to be an exact presentation of data.

Table 2 Unionized* and Nonunionized Organizations by Size

Size of organization by number of employees	Unionized	Nonunionized
500 or fewer	4	3
501 - 3,500	1	8
3,501 - 10,000	2	4
10,001 or more	7	7
TOTALS	14	22

*Unionized covers both labor unions and organized groups of workers.

The case studies are presented in three chapters corresponding to the three major categories of work sharing arrangements identified. Preceding the case studies in each chapter is introductory material giving definitions of the arrangements, a brief historical background, and a description of related legislative activities.

1. Temporary reduction in work hours—short term strategies adopted for a limited time during an economic downturn, with concomitant pay reductions.

- Shortened workweek—all employees in the affected work groups work fewer hours per week and receive less pay.
- Rotation layoff—all affected employees rotate weeks of work with weeks of nonwork, sometimes collecting unemployment insurance benefits for weeks of nonwork.
- Shared Work Unemployment Compensation (SWUC)—an experimental program operating in California which enables workers to be partially compensated through the state unemployment insurance system for temporarily shortened workweeks.

2. Permanent reduction in work hours—arrangements institutionalized in personnel policies and collective bargaining agreements and typically initiated in response to employee desire for shorter work hours and/or longer periods of leisure.

- Shorter workweeks—permanent reductions in the weekly work hours without reduction in pay.
- Part-time—voluntary reduction in total work hours, accompanied by a reduction in salaries and, often, prorated fringe benefits (includes permanent part-time, job sharing, rehiring of retirees, and summer-off arrangements).
- Extended holidays and vacations—substantial increases in employees' leave time, established through changes in personnel policies and collective bargaining arrangements.

3. Flexible worklife options—arrangements developed by employers to provide periodic breaks in worklives of full time employees who meet certain requirements.

- Voluntary time-income trade-off arrangements—contractual arrangements whereby full time employees may, for specific time periods, voluntarily reduce their wages or salaries in exchange for additional time off work.

- Leaves—includes sabbaticals (paid blocks of time away from work to pursue leisure or personal interests) and social service leave (paid time away from the work place to assist nonprofit agencies).
- Phased (or gradual, flexible, transition) retirement—a gradual reduction of work hours for older employees prior to full retirement.

Characteristics and Results of Programs

Work sharing approaches were adopted to meet specific and primary objectives of employers and employees. The following is a list of reasons cited by organizations for initiating work sharing arrangements.

As an alternative to layoffs
To comply with collective bargaining agreements
To prepare for changes in the work force, e.g., increase in number of female employees and/or older workers
To adjust to skill shortages
To meet budgetary restrictions
To retain valuable and skilled workers
Out of concern for individual employees
To enhance community relations
To make recruitment easier
To achieve a more flexible personnel policy
To fill employment requirements
To achieve/maintain production flexibility, e.g., ability to start up more readily as orders increase
To advance affirmative action goals
To improve efficiency and organizational performance
To achieve cost savings
To prevent employee burnout
Out of social responsibility
To prepare employees for retirement

Over time, some employers adapted their programs to meet changing employer and employee needs. For example, a reduced worktime approach designed to mitigate employee burnout subsequently was used to preserve jobs during an economic slump. Another program, initiated to meet tighter budgetary constraints, was made part of the organization's permanent personnel policy because of employees' preferences even when the economic problems did not materialize.

Several common elements characterize successful work sharing arrangements: programs are well planned and carefully defined to meet specific goals; input on the purpose and structure of the program is solicited from management, union officials, and employees; a "let's try and see if it works" attitude pervades the developmental process, resulting in a flexible program design; opportunities for ongoing feedback on the benefits and shortcomings of the program are built into the program structure, making the program more responsive to the organization's goals; and the programs are usually implemented on a small scale, easily manageable basis to provide for a trial and error period.

Precisely because the various work sharing approaches serve diverse needs, organizations that have adopted them have varied in their characteristics. It is neither the specific characteristics of the job or work technology, nor the size of the organization or type of industry, that determines whether an organization will develop work sharing. Rather, two factors seem to influence whether an organization starts a program: organizational climate or a particular business situation.

The two types of organizational climate that characterize the firms in the case studies are: young high-pressured, fast-paced, often high-technology firms for which innovation is a general style; or family-oriented businesses whose approach might be considered paternalistic. Both types of organizations exhibit a special concern for the needs of individuals and a "we care about our employees" philosophy. Other programs are started because of particular business concerns—skill shortages, for example, or economic conditions that would lead to layoffs if no alternatives were offered.

Benefits accrue to employers and employees when work sharing arrangements are implemented under certain conditions, namely when the programs meet specific needs. Most of the problems companies experience with work sharing are administrative in nature: scheduling and coverage difficulties, additional paperwork, more complicated communication, and additional supervision. Little information on costs was available, as few employers had examined the issue in much detail. Although evaluations have not been rigorous in a research sense, employers have been able to determine whether the programs have produced the results for which they were implemented. In those cases, employers felt the benefits outweighed any problems, and many said they saw no need to conduct more rigorous analysis.

Policy Implications

The desire and need for information on work sharing has been apparent from some time. Employers, employees, unions, public policymakers—each group from its own perspective, for its own reasons—have explored the viability of work sharing for dealing with recent social, economic, and demographic trends.

Employers

During the post-World War II era, technological developments and American values and expectations changed at an accelerated rate. In response, corporate management has increasingly sought to develop adaptable, flexible organizational structures that can quickly respond to this changing environment.

Employers are now under pressure to improve organizational performance and productivity as American productivity has declined relative to other countries. The effect of new technology on work design significantly influences worker motivation and performance.

Among the principal changes requiring employers to develop innovative policies are:

- The dramatic increase of women in the workforce and a corresponding increase in dual earner families;
- The changing expectations of workers resulting from the disparity between levels of workers' education and the demands of the labor market;
- The desire of workers for more control over their work and nonwork lives has increased substantially (money and job security no longer acting as the sole motivators of workers);
- The gradual aging of the workforce and the impact of the 1978 Age Discrimination in Employment Act Amendments (which raised the mandatory retirement age to 70 in private organizations and eliminated it in the public sector);
- The declining birth rate and a diminishing supply of younger workers, already resulting in labor shortages in some occupations, clerical and data processing among them.

In the coming decade, human resource development will be integrated with corporate planning and must be in tune with the needs of the organization's top management goals. The more successful organizations will be those which recognize the multiple goals and needs of workers and employers and build flexibility into their management practices. One of the many approaches being considered is new work scheduling arrangements.

Unions

Job preservation and creation remain the highest priority of unions. Traditionally, labor has viewed certain worktime reductions—particularly shorter workweeks without reduction in pay and paid extended holidays, vacations, and other leaves—as one way to achieve these goals. However, with an increasing awareness of the changing needs of their members, some unions are taking a new look at worktime reduction arrangements that represent a departure from their traditional policies.

Union membership has slowed during the past decade. With the growth of the service industry and public sector, there will be a larger pool for recruiting new members, but the needs of these workers may be different from those of union members in blue-collar occupations and trades.

Government

In considering work sharing approaches, public policymakers are responding to current situations and anticipating future needs. The gradual aging of the workforce, persistent unemployment, growing concern about work-family interference, and the technological revolution are issues that public policymakers are addressing. The White House Conference on Families recommended that businesses institute family-oriented personnel policies, including reduced work hour arrangements, as a positive approach to reducing the problems of work-family interference. The effect of science and technology on educational policies is also under review.

Aging. As the percentage of the population aged 65 and older increases (it is conservatively projected to double between 1960 and 2040), the public cost of retirement will increase. Federal expenditures for the elderly—social security, medicare, supplemental security income, and federally financed pensions—made up more than a quarter of the federal budget in 1979. With a growing elderly population, the share of budget expenditures will also rise.

The decreasing ratio of workers who contribute to retired beneficiaries of social security may affect the solvency of the social security fund. Currently, three workers contribute to the fund for every retired beneficiary; in 2020, two workers will support one beneficiary. Workers in the ''baby boom'' generation will begin turning 65 in 2010 at about the time the productive working population for the country will be shrinking in relative size (assuming relatively little change in the current birth rate). By 2020, there will be only 3.5 working age Americans for every person aged 65 as against today's 5 workers to every person over 65. High inflation and unemployment over the past decade have also resulted in reduced contributions to the social security fund.

Public policy recommendations have been made to extend the eligibility age at which retirees receive full social security benefits. The President's Commission on Pension Policy recommends an increase in the normal retirement age to 68, to be phased in over a 12-year period beginning in 1990.[3] Legislation has been introduced in the U.S. House of Representatives by Representative Claude Pepper (D-FL) to provide incentives for older workers to remain in the workforce. An identical provision in two bills, H.R. 3396 and H.R. 3397, would require employers to continue benefit accrual for employees up to age 70. H.R. 3397 would also

3. *Coming of Age: Toward a National Retirement Income Policy* Washington, DC: President's Commission on Pension Policy, February 1981.

abolish mandatory retirement. The bills have been jointly referred to the House Committees on Ways and Means and Education and Labor. Another recommendation by the President's Commission on Pension Policy is for development of research and demonstration programs on alternative work schedules for older workers.

The policy questions raised are: Would such financial incentives as tax credits or cost reimbursements encourage employers to adopt phased retirement programs? To what extent will the adoption of phased retirement programs by a greater number of companies extend the worklives of older workers, particularly in light of proposed changes in social security, inflation, and enforcement of the Age Discrimination in Employment Act Amendments?

Employment. In the past, discussion of work sharing has received serious attention during recessionary periods as a short term strategy to deal with unemployment. Temporary reduced work hour approaches have gained considerable momentum during such periods of economic decline. However, as the case studies illustrate, work sharing in its broadest sense could also offer an effective strategy to deal with problems of long term unemployment.

Changing and interacting economic, social, and demographic conditions make forecasting labor force composition difficult. Nevertheless, their cumulative impact coupled with the persistent failure of the U.S. economy to create full employment have forced the realization that long term unemployment is becoming an overriding societal concern. In confronting this issue, policymakers are now taking a serious look at the possibilities of adjusting worktime to increase job opportunities. Work sharing may even help alleviate the conflicts and strains created by intense competition for jobs. In several cases, programs have already been initiated.

There are other signs that work sharing policies affect a variety of interests. Historically, unions have pressed for extended time away from work—longer vacations or paid personal holidays, for example—as a way to increase employment opportunities. The continued growth in part-time employment may be attributed in part to a need by some employees for greater flexibility. In recent years, some employers have offered summer-off programs for parents with school-age children.

However, the implications of work sharing as public policy have not been fully explored. While various work sharing programs benefit different population segments, an assessment of their aggregate effect—benefits and costs—on society is needed.

The policy questions raised are: Will reduced hour schedules encourage a greater number of people to enter the workforce, thereby increasing competition for fewer jobs? Will the growth of reduced work hour arrangements adversely affect the employment possibilities of people requiring full-time work and full-time compensation? Are there people now employed full time who would willingly trade income for additional leisure time, thereby opening up employment opportunities? Will spreading the work over a larger group of workers promote the broader goals of extending equal employment opportunity and safeguarding affirmative action gains? Does work sharing improve productivity? Will the policy emphasis on work sharing divert attention from the development of other monetary and fiscal policies that promote growth and job creation or help focus it?

Background of this Study

The Employment and Training Division of the U.S. Department of Labor became interested in work sharing approaches, partially as a way to deal with inflation and persistently high unemployment, and recognized the need for information that would allow employers to assess the feasibility of such approaches. As a result, the Department of Labor (DOL) awarded a grant to the National Council for Alternative Work Patterns (NCAWP), a national nonprofit research and resource center in Washington, D.C., to study work sharing in organizations in the United States.

NCAWP conducted an extensive search to identify organizations that had started work sharing programs. Questionnaires were then mailed to those organizations, requesting information about their programs, their reasons for starting them, the number of participants, their formal and informal evaluations, and demographic information about the company (such as size, type of industry, composition of workforce, and unionization of workers). From a pool of 130 responses, NCAWP identified a number of organizations for more detailed study. Several considerations guided our selection. One goal was to examine as great a variety of programs as possible. Beyond that, we wanted to look at programs in a variety of settings—large and small companies in different types of industries, employing different technologies, and nonunionized as well as unionized workers. Geographic locations also guided our choice. A final but important consideration was the employers' program design.

NCAWP then conducted on-site interviews to explore in greater detail: the reasons for starting the programs; who had made the decisions; what the organizational philosophy and climate had been; how the program had been developed and communicated to workers; the extent of union involvement in initiating, developing, and implementing the program; the implementation steps; the special considerations and how they had been handled; how compensation had been administered; the difficulties encountered, benefits accrued, and changes the organization would make if it were to start over; how the program had been evaluated; the response of workers; the impact on families and the community; the unanticipated outcomes; and whether the program had met its objectives.

We spoke with senior executives, line managers, human resource and personnel staff, benefits and compensation analysts, union representatives, government officials, and employees in an attempt to gain the broadest perspective on the development and impact of these approaches.

The case studies presented in this book represent the culmination of these efforts. Not all companies identified as having work sharing programs and subsequently interviewed are described in the case studies. We have tried to include a diversity of organizations in various parts of the country that started these programs for a variety of reasons.

1
TEMPORARY REDUCTION
IN WORK HOURS

Temporary reduction in work hours as an alternative to layoffs is perhaps the most widely known form of work sharing. While the shortened workweek is the most common form of this work sharing approach, there are two other distinct arrangements—rotation layoff and short-time compensation.

Commitment to job security and practical operational considerations which do not make layoffs feasible are among the reasons some employers have turned to temporary work hour reductions with concomitant pay reductions during an economic downturn. Although the short term costs may be greater because the employer continues to pay full fringe benefits while employees work less time, temporary work hour reductions do offer benefits that make the programs cost-effective for some employers over the long run. Reduced work hour arrangements enable employers to retain skilled workers during a slack period, avoid additional rehiring and retraining costs, and improve morale. However, if the economic downturn lasts substantially longer than expected and ultimately requires a layoff, the short term benefits may be offset.

Historical Perspective

Reducing work hours temporarily to combat joblessness is not a new strategy. During the Depression, when there was no unemployment insurance to help people who were out of work, many companies, in cooperation with their employees, avoided laying off some workers by sharing the available work among all workers on a reduced workweek (reduced salary) basis. For example, an employer could reduce the work hours of all employees by 20 percent rather than lay off 20 percent of the existing workforce.

Since the 1930s, the development of the unemployment insurance (UI) system and provisions of collective bargaining agreements have made it economically beneficial to employers to invoke a layoff rather than develop alternative approaches. Some employers are prevented by collective bargaining agreements from instituting a shortened work hour option. However, a 1974 study conducted by Peter Henle for the Congressional Research Service found that even when collective bargaining agreements include provisions for reduced work hours during a production slowdown (one out of every five major agreements), these provisions are rarely invoked except in the highly unstable garment industry.[1] From the unions' perspective, work sharing means a sharing of unemployment.

Today, unlike the 1930s when a layoff meant impoverishment, laid off workers receive income support through the unemployment insurance system. Workers whose unions have negotiated supplemental benefits for layoff periods may receive a portion of their lost income, in some instances replacing up to 90 percent of their normal take-home pay. Depending on their individual skills, financial situation, workforce solidarity, and the local labor market, some workers may prefer a layoff to a temporary work hour reduction.

---

1. Peter Henle, *Work Sharing as an Alternative to Layoffs,* Washington: Congressional Research Service, Library of Congress, 1976.

However, the major impediment to wider consideration of temporary reductions in worktime is the structure of the existing unemployment insurance system. Until 1978, no state permitted the payment of unemployment benefits to workers unemployed for only one day a week. While all states permit partial compensation, the method for determining the amount of benefits is, in reality, not suited for slightly shorter workweeks. In most states, partial compensation is tied to the worker's weekly benefit amount (WBA) under a full week of unemployment and is limited to the difference between the WBA and the income earned during the week. For example, if an employee earns $200 for a 40-hour workweek and is eligible to receive $75 in benefits for a week of unemployment, the worker could not receive benefits for a 32-hour workweek because the earnings for more than two days of work would exceed $75.

Despite these disincentives—the current structure of the UI system, provisions of collective bargaining agreements, employee concerns, and company costs—some companies have responded to a general economic or industry-specific downturn by temporarily reducing work hours. Once they have analyzed the long-run costs of a layoff, these companies have concluded that a temporary reduction in hours is a more cost-effective strategy. In addition to the benefits of retaining skilled workers, avoiding additional rehiring and retraining costs, improving morale, safeguarding affirmative action gains, and realizing community good will, reduced work hours enable companies to schedule production with greater flexibility as demand fluctuates and to maintain the ability to satisfy customers once business improves. These arrangements also enable companies to maintain productivity by obviating the need of senior workers to invoke "bumping privileges" and transfer to jobs for which their skills are not current.

Senior workers have agreed to participate in these reduced work hour arrangements when the approach is used for a short period. The arrangements often provide for continuation of fringe benefits and for reductions in work-related costs, such as transportation, lunch, and child care. Further, senior workers have enjoyed the extra time off to pursue various activities; in some settings, they have felt a commitment to younger workers in their work groups. When reductions continue for a longer time than anticipated, however, senior workers who would be unaffected by layoffs have questioned the equity of these arrangements.

Shortened Workweek

In a shortened workweek, all employees in the affected work groups work fewer hours per week and receive less pay. This is the most common short term strategy for avoiding a layoff.[2] During the 1974-75 recession, for example, New York Telephone and the Telephone Traffic Union agreed to a 4-day workweek—with a 20 percent salary reduction—for 2,000 operators in order to save the jobs of 400 employees.

More recently, in April 1980, 45 employees of the Rental and Operations Unit of the Portland, Oregon Housing Authority requested a 32-hour workweek as an alternative to a proposed 20 percent reduction of staff.

Rotation Layoff

Rotation layoff is an arrangement whereby all affected employees rotate weeks of work with weeks of nonwork. Companies have developed this approach to short term economic slumps in order to minimize the economic impact

2. In the case studies in this chapter, we have focused on innovative approaches which provide partial compensation in temporarily reduced work hour arrangements.

on workers rather than summarily lay them off. Rotation layoff enables workers to collect unemployment insurance benefits for weeks of nonwork.

The rotation cycle may vary from alternating weeks of work with weeks of layoff to one week of layoff out of a longer cycle—one in four weeks, for example. Depending on production demands and type of operation, all employees in an affected unit may be on layoff at the same time (this approach has been used when operations require that machinery be run with all employees present) or only a portion may be on layoff at a time.

Short-Time Compensation

In recent years, American public policymakers have begun to seriously explore modification of the unemployment insurance system to permit partial compensation for temporarily reduced workweeks. Known as short-time compensation (STC), shared work compensation (SWC), and shared work unemployment compensation (SWUC), this approach has been used in Europe since the 1920s and has become more widespread since the economic crisis of the mid-1970s.

Short-time compensation differs from other employment policies in that its goal is to enable employers to retain workers when faced with economic downturns perceived as temporary. The research agenda on shared-work compensation developed by Mathematica Policy Research lists key questions that warrant serious consideration.

1. What are the social-efficiency implications of SWC in the short-run? In the long-run?
2. What are the equity implications of SWC? In particular, what are its distributional consequences?
3. Which workers would prefer SWC to the current UI program? What are their personal characteristics? What are their job characteristics?

4. How will SWC participation affect income, nonwage benefits, and other aspects of workers' well-being?
5. What forms of compensation and/or special provisions will labor organizations bargain for in response to the possible use of SWC?
6. To what extent will hours adjustments be used instead of employment adjustments? Will SWC lead to greater or smaller labor-service adjustments?
7. How will the timing of labor-service adjustments—for both downturns and upturns—be affected by SWC?
8. What will the productivity consequences of SWC be in the short-run? In the long-run?
9. What are the costs of SWC and how do they compare to the current UI program? How are these costs distributed to business, labor, and others?
10. How will SWC integrate administratively into the current UI program? What rule changes are necessary or desirable?[3]

Discussion of this approach was brought to the forefront in 1975 when the New York City Commission on Civil Rights began to explore feasible ways to reduce joblessness resulting from the city's budget problems. The Commission was concerned with finding approaches that would minimize the loss of affirmative action gains and sponsored a conference on alternatives to layoffs. Eleanor Holmes Norton, at that time chair of the Commission, considered the idea of "work sharing subsidized with unemployment insurance. . . one of the most promising and practical alternatives to unemployment."

With the support of the New York State AFL-CIO, an amendment was introduced in 1976 into the New York State

---

3. Stuart Kerachsky, Walter Corson, and Walter Nicholson, *Shared-Work Compensation: A Research Agenda* prepared by Mathematica Policy Research, Inc. for the Office of Research and Development, Employment and Training Administration, U.S. Department of Labor, 1981.

Legislature by Representative Seymour Posner (D) to permit a change in the unemployment insurance regulations. However, the bill died in committee.

Since the mid-1970s, federal government interest in shared work as a means to stabilize employment has grown at a slow but steady rate. In 1978, the U.S. Department of Labor (DOL) established a special task force to monitor existing programs in Canada and Western Europe. In addition, the Employment and Training Administration, DOL, sponsored an exploratory survey designed to assess the reaction of labor, business, and other groups to the concept. The results of this study and a report of the activities of the DOL task force will be included in a forthcoming publication by the Unemployment Insurance Service, Office of Research, Legislation and Program Policy, DOL, as part of the UI Occasional Papers series.

During June 1980, U.S. Representative Patricia Schroeder (D-CO) introduced legislation into the 96th Congress, 2nd Session, that would encourage shared work as an alternative to layoffs. The Short Time Compensation Act of 1980 (H.R. 7529) would authorize the Secretary of Labor to develop model legislation, make grants, and provide technical assistance to states interested in developing this type of approach. Representative Schroeder reintroduced the bill (H.R. 3005) in the 97th Congress is a somewhat modified form.

Because of economic conditions, there is renewed interest at the state level in shared work unemployment insurance benefit programs as a way of providing an alternative to layoffs during periods of economic downturn. The Arizona state legislature passed shared work unemployment legislation (S. 1005) in April 1981. Legislation (S. 328) was reported favorably out of the Oregon Senate in February 1981, but no further action has been taken. New York's

Governor, Hugh Carey, in his 1981 general economic package, proposed that New York State adopt a pilot shared work compensation plan. Although legislation was introduced (S. 5304), it was not enacted during the past session. A number of other states have introduced related legislation since the start of 1981—Illinois (H. 1286, April), Maryland (H.1621, February), and Hawaii (H. 1926, February)—but have not taken action. In Maine, a bill (H. 1012) was introduced, but was withdrawn by the state House and Senate.

Experimental California SWUC Program

The State of California, in anticipation of widespread layoffs resulting from the passage of Proposition 13, passed legislation introduced by Senator Bill Green (D) which established a statewide Shared Work Unemployment Compensation experimental program. Although the massive layoffs of public employees did not materialize, the program was nonetheless implemented in July 1978. Extended by legislation in July 1979, SWUC permits employers facing a business downturn to choose a reduction in the hours and wages of all or a part of their workforce instead of layoffs. Recent legislation (S. 130) passed by the California Senate in May 1981 would extend the program to 1983. No action has been taken by the California House to date.

The program operates within California's existing unemployment insurance system, and is administered by the California Employment Development Department (EDD). (A detailed description of the California SWUC program administrative procedures appears on pages 48-51 preceding case studies of three SWUC programs.) In order for companies to participate in SWUC, at least 10 percent of their employees must be affected. The reduction must result in at least a 10 percent cutback in hours and wages. Employer participation is voluntary; however, if employees are covered by collective bargaining agreements, their union must agree to the plan.

The program permits payment of partial benefits for up to 20 weeks during a 52-week period. In many cases, employees may receive about 90 percent of their regular salaries for a normal workweek. If workers are laid off after the 20 weeks are used up, they are eligible for regular unemployment insurance benefits, but the benefits are reduced slightly to reflect the dollar costs of the SWUC benefits already received.

The typical worktime reduction among participating firms has been 20 percent with more than two-thirds of the firms reducing their workweek from five days to four. Participating employees filed claims for an average of five weeks.

Employer interest started out quite slowly when the SWUC program first began in July 1978, with only 15 plans submitted and approved during the first six months of the program. However, by September 1979, as reported by Fred Best and James Mattesich in the *Monthly Labor Review,*[4] 312 employers were approved. Significant increases occurred during 1980. A preliminary report on SWUC, *A Review of the Shared Work Unemployment Compensation Program,* prepared by the California Office of the Legislative Analyst (OLA), indicated that as of October 1980, 1,293 work sharing plans had been approved.

The OLA report notes that employers in the manufacturing sector (where unemployment rates have been higher than average) make relatively greater use of SWUC than other industries; and employers in the general sector, restaurants, hotels, and the public sector (where unemployment is lower than average) make less use of SWUC.

Participating firms typically have been small. Close to 64 percent of the SWUC employers, according to the

4. Fred Best and James Mattesich, "Short-Time Compensation Systems in California and Europe," *Monthly Labor Review, July 1980.*

Legislative Analyst figures, have between 10 and 250 employees. As of June 1980, approximately 22 percent of all employees approved to participate in SWUC, though not necessarily union members, work for unionized employers.

Through September 1980, 35,300 employees were approved participants in SWUC. OLA analyzed a sample of 4,786 SWUC claimants to ascertain participant characteristics and concluded that the distribution of SWUC claimants by sex is fairly similar to the national unemployment statistics, while the distributions by age and race are significantly different. Nonwhites comprise about 45 percent of SWUC claimants, whereas on the national level this group represents about 11 percent of the employed labor force and 22 percent of the unemployed labor force. National figures indicate that 25 percent of all unemployed persons are under 20 years old; however, only 3 percent of SWUC claimants are in this age group.

Costs. A rigorous cost-benefit analysis of the impact of SWUC on firms, employees, and the unemployment fund is currently underway at EDD. Among the factors that employers must weigh are continuation of fringe benefits and payroll taxes (UI and social security), reduction in wages paid to higher earning workers, and decreases in rehiring and retraining costs as well as the impact of SWUC on the firm's UI experience rating. In discussions with OLA, employers indicated that other considerations that are not easily quantifiable, such as the ability to expand output more readily when orders increase and their commitment to the job security of their workers, need to be included in the equation.

The cost impact on employees depends on the amount of partial compensation available under SWUC. For some workers, the replacement rate may be more than 90 percent. The highest paid workers receive a lower percentage of take-home pay because they are constrained by the ceiling on UI benefits. (See Appendix for a schedule of California benefit amounts.) Participants also save on reduced work-related expenses such as food and transportation.

The Legislative Analyst report notes that it is difficult to draw any conclusions at this time on the impact of the SWUC program on the UI fund as data is still being collected. The report includes models developed by Best and Mattesich that show the variables under which the net costs to the UI fund could increase or decrease. In order to demonstrate the potential cost difference between SWUC and regular UI, the OLA reported that through September 1980, $1.8 million was paid out in SWUC benefits while regular UI payments for 1981 alone are estimated at $1.4 billion. An interim report evaluating the program costs and other effects of SWUC on employers and employees during its first year of use was released June 1981, and the final evaluation is scheduled to be released in December 1981.

ROTATION LAYOFF

Fieldcrest Mills, Inc.

Fieldcrest had its beginning in 1898 when industrialist and town builder Benjamin Frank Mebane set out to build a textile mill a year. While he proceeded almost on schedule—6 mills in 8 years in what is now Eden, North Carolina—the mills had financial difficulties and were acquired between 1905 and 1912 by Marshall Fields and Company, a heavy investor. Marshall Fields expanded and improved the mills and also contributed to the development of the community by repairing streets, putting up lights, improving sanitation, and expanding the limited recreational facilities.

In 1953, Fieldcrest was purchased by a new, independent corporation, Fieldcrest Mills, Inc., which has followed an active program of construction, expansion, and acquisition. The company manufactures and markets a variety of textile products for the home (Fieldcrest and St. Mary's bed and bath products and Karastan, carpets and rugs), performs commission finishing, and manufactures yarn for other textile companies.

Hourly production workers make up more than 11,000 of Fieldcrest Mills' workforce of 13,000 in its 26 plants in five southeastern states. Approximately 53 percent of the production employees (and, likewise, of the total workforce) are male.

Fieldcrest Mills is one of the largest industries in North Carolina. Corporate headquarters is at Eden, where the firm's operations are concentrated. Eden's economy is based on Fieldcrest Mills manufacturing, tobacco farming and, to a lesser extent, other industries. Many families earn their living by combining tobacco farming and working at an industrial job.

Most Fieldcrest Mills workers are unionized and for the past 40 years have been represented by the Amalgamated Clothing and Textile Workers, AFL-CIO. (Before the clothing and textile unions merged, Fieldcrest bargained with the Textile Workers Union.) The bargaining unit at one plant is the independent United Textile Workers.

Decisionmaking

Fieldcrest Mills has had record sales and earnings for the past several years and, even during the 1974-75 recession, has expanded. However, the nature of the industry is such that Fieldcrest Mills' production demands frequently vary from plant to plant and year to year, sometimes requiring cutbacks in work hours or jobs. Most downturn periods are relatively short, ranging from a few weeks to a few months (although one lasted a year). Even so, there is concern over losing skilled workers during these downturns—to other companies or to other Fieldcrest plants which compete for talented workers.

In seeking an acceptable alternative to layoffs during the temporary downturns, the company and union have developed a reduced work hour plan, referred to as a "sendout." Employees either work rotating weeks on and off, shorter days, or shorter weeks, sometimes collecting unemployment insurance compensation (depending on how hours are reduced). For example, employees working rotating on-off weeks collect unemployment insurance during the weeks off.

Management at Fieldcrest Mills prefers sendouts to layoffs as a short term solution. According to Regional Personnel Manager R.L. Moore, sendouts provide production flexibility and efficiency. All or only some of the production workers in a plant may be involved, depending on the nature of the operation. Selection of employees is based on machine schedules, not on seniority.

Provided the sendout is short term, the affected unions also view this approach favorably. To protect seniority rights, the union negotiated a provision in the collective bargaining agreement that limits sendout periods. The union-management bargaining agreement provides that:

> During slack periods work may, at the discretion of the plant, be shared by all employees on the operations until the hours of work of such employees who are sharing the work fall below 32 hours per week for 4 consecutive weeks, at which time layoffs shall be made according to the seniority provisions of the Section. Should the hours of work fall below 24 hours per week for 2 consecutive weeks, a layoff shall be made. . . .

Employee Response

There are a number of reasons senior workers are willing to participate in sendouts. One is partial compensation, in some instances, for loss of income. However, even when unemployment compensation is not provided, many senior employees participate because:

- They enjoy extra time off from work for such activities as farming, hunting, fishing, and family.
- A portion of the income loss is offset by certain cost savings. For example, Fieldcrest Mills pays the employee's 50 percent share of life and health insurance premiums during sendouts and continues to provide holiday pay. (These entitlements are not provided during layoff.) Workers also save on work related costs, such as transportation and lunch.
- Employees sometimes can arrange to be off at times most suitable to their needs, through an informal trade-off system. Those who prefer to work full time are permitted to seek a substitute (who must be approved by the plant foreman or manager).
- Employees may seek transfers to other company facilities if the loss of income under sendout becomes burdensome. (Since production demand varies from plant to plant, jobs often are available at one facility while another experiences a downturn and workforce reduction.)
- Traditional "small town" relationships and attitudes, that is, long-standing friendships, a sense of fair play, and a desire to help others, are significant.

When sendouts last for an extended period, problems—mainly financial—arise for workers. Weekly income losses mount and those fringe benefits tied to annual earnings begin to be adversely affected. For example, the vacation benefit, a lump sum amount representing a percentage of an employee's annual earnings, decreases. Retirement benefits also are affected, since they are based on career earnings.

Moore reports that union officials accept work sharing so long as participating senior workers do not complain. When senior workers become dissatisfied, they ask union leaders to invoke the layoff provision as soon as the contractual limit for sendouts is reached. The weeks immediately after the contractual limit is reached are critical, according to Moore; if the union doesn't invoke layoffs during that time, it is unlikely to do so for a while. Moore's experience has been that senior employees have tolerated sendouts for extended periods beyond the limit. The union seldom has invoked the layoff provision.

Effect on Management

The costs of absorbing the workers' share of life and health insurance and paying other fringe benefits such as holidays do mount during lengthy sendouts. At some point, these costs outweigh advantages.

As a short term solution, however, sendouts do provide production flexibility—an important management consideration in an operation as large and varied as Fieldcrest. For example, in the blanket mill, where efficient operation requires running machines at full capacity with everyone working, the plant closes for one week and is in operation the next. In blanket finishing, where operations are tied to customer deliveries, the plant might operate on short days or short weeks. Operations are not highly integrated in the bedspread plant, so part of the plant operates on a sendout while remaining departments operate at full capacity or on overtime. Plants operating with three shifts can rotate so that an employee will be off one week out of three.

Unemployment Insurance Compensation

Eligibility for unemployment insurance compensation and level of benefits depend on the work sharing arrangement of the sendout. Therefore, it is difficult for the company to generalize about, for example, the income loss to a senior employee on work sharing who otherwise would be working full time. Dorothy Tredway, Branch Manager of North Carolina's Employment Security Office, describes the North Carolina program as follows:

- There are three unemployment categories under which an individual can receive benefits.
  (1) Total unemployment: Worker has lost his/her job connection, is entirely out of work, and receives no wages;
  (2) Part-time unemployment: Worker has lost his/her regular employment but has earnings from odd jobs

less than the eligibility cutoff amount;

(3) Partial unemployment (temporary layoff): Worker retains his/her job connection but, due to lack of work, is employed less than the equivalent of three full-time days (or less than 24 hours) during a payroll week and earns less than the eligibility cutoff amount. A worker can be totally unemployed (no earnings) for up to four consecutive weeks and will be listed in this category.

• All persons receiving unemployment insurance benefits must be seeking employment except persons who are receiving benefits under the partial unemployment category.

• A worker eligible for unemployment insurance benefits under one of the three types of unemployment categories must forego receiving benefits one week during the calendar year, known as the waiting period.

• Unemployment insurance benefits are considered taxable income when filing federal and state tax returns.

• To qualify for unemployment insurance an individual must have been employed during a base period, defined as the first four of the last five calendar quarters preceding the quarter in which the initial claim is filed.

• The weekly benefit is calculated from the highest quarter during the base period.

The average hourly straight time wage at Fieldcrest Mills was $5.48 as of December 1980. At this wage, a fully laid off worker would receive a weekly benefit of $110. A partially unemployed worker receiving $5.48 an hour could earn approximately 20 percent of the weekly benefits, or $22, before benefits are reduced dollar for dollar. Therefore, the maximum this employee could earn on a combination of wages and unemployment insurance benefits is $132. (After reaching $132, or the employee's weekly benefit amount plus earnings allowance, unemployment insurance benefits cease.)

Table 3 gives examples of income loss under various work sharing schedules:

Table 3   Income Loss Under Work Sharing

No. of hours of work at $5.48/hour	Work sharing income	Full-time income	Weekly income loss
30 hrs/week wages	$164	$219	$55
Ineligible for UI	---		
20 hrs/week wages	110		
UI benefit allowance	22		
	132	219	87
16 hrs/week wages	88		
UI benefit allowance	44		
	132	219	87
Rotation one week on/off	219	219	
40 hrs/week wages (week #1)			
UI benefit allowance (week #2)	110	219	
	329	438	
Average 2 week period	$165/week	$219/week	$54
Rotation 1 week off/2 weeks on:			
UI benefit allowance (week #1)	110	219	
40 hrs/week wages (week #2)	219	219	
40 hrs/week wages (week #3)	219	219	
	548	657	
Average 3 week period	$183	$219	$36

To facilitate the benefit claims process during sendouts, Fieldcrest initiates the unemployment insurance benefit claim process by giving a completed temporary layoff claim form for each employee on sendout to the Eden branch of the North Carolina Employment Security office. Employment Security staff then assign appointment dates for employees to appear at the office to file their claims.

Tredway reported that employees from other manufacturing and construction firms in the area receive benefits under the partial unemployment category. She noted that more than 50 percent of weeks of unemployment claims in the Eden branch are from individuals in the partial unemployment category, that is, from individuals attached to a job.

ROTATION LAYOFF

American Velvet

American Velvet is a textile manufacturing firm privately owned since 1892 by the Wimpheimer family. Its 330 employees are represented by the Amalgamated Clothing and Textile Workers Union, AFL-CIO, Local 110T. About 65 percent of the workforce is male; one-third of the production workers are female. Base pay ranges from $4.43 to $6.50 an hour. While the standard workweek is 40 hours, production workers average a 6-day, 48-hour workweek.

Located in Stonington, Connecticut, in the less populated southeastern section of the state, American Velvet faces competition for skilled personnel from several large companies in neighboring Groton and New London. The largest of these has contracts with the U.S. Navy to build submarines.

Decisionmaking

During the 1974-75 recession, orders to American Velvet decreased sharply, reducing the need for skilled workers in the weaving department. Since these highly skilled workers gain much of their expertise through on-the-job training and the department was staffed with newly trained young employees at the time, company president Jacques Wimpheimer was particularly concerned about their imminent layoff. In addition, management in this small, family-owned company is committed to employee job security.

Management met with the 9-person union negotiating team to develop alternative approaches to layoff. The strategy developed by this joint labor-management committee was a rotational layoff—a system of alternating one week of work with one week of layoff.

The union called a special membership meeting to explain the plan and win ratification. Working within a favorable labor-management climate, employees wanted to help the company retain skilled workers so it could remain competitive during the recession, and they ratified the plan. Although they would not have been affected by the layoff, senior workers supported the rotational layoff out of concern for junior workers.

Program

Between December 1974 and September 1975, approximately 300 employees participated in the rotational layoff plan. Initially intended only for weavers, the program was extended to all production workers and some foremen as the recession continued.

The company sent a letter describing the arrangement to all employees. Shop stewards and foremen in each department were responsible for setting rotation schedules. In some departments, employees worked one week and the department closed the next. In other departments, operations required that the schedules be staggered, with half the employees working one week and the other half the following week.

Tied to the Connecticut unemployment insurance (UI) system, employees collected UI benefits during layoff weeks, beginning with the first week of layoff as Connecticut does not have a waiting period. The result was that employees were partially compensated for the loss of wages. Additionally, they continued to receive full fringe benefits from the company.

To ease the burden on employees of having to report to the UI office each week to collect benefits, company officials worked with local UI representatives to establish a procedure for processing UI claims whereby the company bore the responsibility. American Velvet collected the UI forms from all eligible employees and mailed them to the UI office which, in turn, sent the benefit checks directly to the employees.

The program was discontinued in September 1975, when the unemployment insurance benefit period ended. The company found the program costly and, since the need to reduce production continued, was forced to return to a traditional arrangement and lay off workers.

Effect on Employees

The rotational layoff arrangement allowed junior workers to retain their jobs and fringe benefits. Since the area's economy was experiencing a business slowdown, many workers felt it would have been difficult to find new jobs. They appreciated the company's efforts to develop an alternative to layoffs that saved their jobs.

Senior workers initially supported the program. They enjoyed the leisure time, for which they were partially compensated. However, as the rotational layoff wore on, senior workers began to question the equity of the work sharing approach: they would not have been affected by a layoff, yet they were receiving reduced incomes under this plan. Resentment began to surface, but the issue became moot because the program soon was terminated as the UI benefit period was exhausted.

Effect on Employer

According to company officials, the potential advantage of retaining skilled junior workers made the rotational layoff plan attractive. Management believed the cost of continuing fringe benefits could be offset by later savings resulting from not having to recruit and train replacements for laid off employees who found jobs elsewhere. However, the downturn in orders lasted longer than anticipated. By the time the UI benefit period ended, orders had not increased sufficiently to justify recalling the entire workforce to full-time employment, and the company laid off some workers, including weavers. When production demands eventually increased, some of the laid off workers were not available to return to American Velvet. Thus, the company incurred both the hiring and training expenses it had tried to avoid through the adoption of rotational layoffs, and the cost of fringe benefits during the rotational layoff. Most significantly to the company, the rotational layoff plan affected American Velvet's UI experience rating, which increased dramatically from 2.7 percent to more than 6 percent, thereby raising the company's UI contribution.

Conclusion

There is agreement among management that the company's effort to save jobs generated good will for American Velvet among employees, union leaders, and the community. But, because of the length of the program, rotational layoff was costly to the company. President Wimpheimer believes that a short term work sharing approach can be beneficial to firms in some circumstances. He cautions that limitations must be set and the program's cost/benefit ratio must be monitored carefully.

ROTATION LAYOFF

Tomkins-Johnson Division
Aeroquip Corporation

Tomkins-Johnson (T-J) has been manufacturing cylinders since 1923. Approximately 320 of the company's 400 employees work out of the Jackson, Michigan headquarters office. It also operates production facilities in Decatur, Alabama and White City, Oregon.

In 1979, T-J became a division of another Jackson-based company, Aeroquip, which manufactures a wide range of products for the fluid power industry, including hose and fittings for industrial, automotive, aircraft, and marine fluid power applications. In turn, the Aeroquip group, comprised of 6,000 employees in 14 states and 11 foreign countries, is a wholly owned subsidiary of the Libby-Owens-Ford Company in Toledo, Ohio.

Jackson, Michigan is a highly industrialized small city with a population of 100,000. Manufacturing in Jackson, which is a 1.5-hour drive from Detroit, is related to the auto industry to a considerable extent. While nearly all of the area's manufacturers are unionized, T-J employees are not represented by a union.

Early in September 1979, customer orders at T-J decreased. Management forecast an increase in orders by the end of the year, but concluded that over the next four months the production workforce would have to be reduced by 20 employees. To avoid laying off the 20 employees, management decided to take an alternate approach, which T-J refers to as rotation layoffs. The effect was to share the burden of work reduction among 80 employees. The employees were divided into four groups of 20, with each group rotating one week of layoff out of a 4-week cycle during the 4-month period. During their week on layoff, employees received unemployment insurance benefits.

Before the effects on company and employees—perceived as favorable by both groups—and the operation of the program are described, T-J's use of this approach during the 1974-75 recession should be reviewed. At that time, according to management, it was a "cost effective and employee-acceptable" alternative to traditional methods of dealing with economic down cycles. Not insignificant in its search for alternative methods was the pattern of stable employment in the company; there had been few major workforce reductions since the company's beginning.

During the 1974-75 recession, business declined substantially and T-J was forced to reduce its workforce by 60 employees. As sales continued to drop, T-J faced further need to reduce its workforce. This second phase would have required laying off many of T-J's most senior and skilled machinists and technicians. Management was concerned that it might not be able to regain these workers once business picked up and they were needed again. Further, management hoped to minimize the economic impact on these workers, whose well-being also was of concern. (This interest is evidenced at T-J by the stamping of cylinders with the personal mark of the workers who assemble them and the inspectors, for the dual purpose of maintaining accountability and instilling worker pride.)

Decisionmaking

The idea of rotation layoff came during a management brainstorming session. The approach had not been "heard of or tried before," according to an article by former Corporate Personnel Director William Homjak in the September 1978 *Personnel Administrator*. It seemed a way to avoid problems with other approaches discussed, such as a shorter workweek which would provide for no unemployment benefits because of the existing structure of the unemployment insurance system. After discussing the plan with operations management, checking the feasibility, and receiving cooperation from the Michigan Employment Security Commission, T-J began the new program.

1975 Program

More than 160 employees, production and maintenance employees as well as office personnel, participated in the 1975 program. At the main Jackson facility, it began on September 1, 1975 and ended December 31, 1975. The program also ran four months at the Oregon and Alabama facilities, but at different times.

Each participating employee was laid off for one week, worked three weeks, then was laid off again for one week, and so on, over the four-month period. Participants continued to receive full fringe benefits. Job security, seniority, and merit systems were not affected.

A schedule of layoff weeks and workweeks, as well as information on anticipated program length, was distributed to each participating employee at the beginning of the program.

In 1977, T-J conducted a comprehensive employee opinion survey at its main Jackson plant. Included was a question soliciting the employees opinions about the rotation layoff program. The responses of the approximately 290 employees who answered the question confirmed earlier, informal observations that employees were positive about the program:

- 91.5 percent of employees who had participated in the program favored the program;
- 94 percent of first line supervisors who had been affected by the program favored it;
- 91 percent of all management groups favored the program;
- 81.4 percent of all employees working at the main facility favored the program.

Management attributed the defeat of a union organizing drive in 1978 by a 3 to 1 margin to strong employee feelings that the company had tried to help them rather than summarily lay them off.

1979 Program

With this good response to the approach behind them, management decided to reinstitute the rotation layoff when T-J again faced a down production cycle in 1979. Personnel management met with personnel of the Michigan Employment Security Commission (MESC) in September 1979 to discuss policy and procedures for processing unemployment insurance claims. It was agreed at that meeting that:

- T-J must furnish MESC with a list of personnel who would be participating in the rotation, including names, social security numbers, and dates of layoffs; and

- T-J must distribute registration forms to rotating employees the week preceding their layoff (necessary only once a year for each participant).

Also clarified at that meeting were such things as the amount of unemployment insurance which would be available, what information needed to be reported by employees to MESC, and how employees would process claims.

The rotation layoff period began in October 1979. At the end of the second cycle, when future needs were uncertain but management anticipated a longer layoff period than originally planned, all employees—both those on rotation and those working full time—were asked their opinions about maintaining, reducing, or increasing the rotation pool or relying on layoffs.

Employee response was overwhelmingly in favor of increasing the rotation pool, with nine out of ten supporting this change. While the questionnaire was regarded as a preference poll rather than a vote on policy, T-J did continue the program.

Differences Between the 1975 and 1979 Programs

In 1975, all categories of workers participated in the rotation layoffs. Since the 1979-80 business downturn wasn't as severe as in 1975, nonproduction workers were exempt. When T-J sent its survey to employees in 1979, production workers expressed displeasure about management's decision to exclude office personnel.

Another difference was administrative. In 1975, the firm processed the unemployment claims at the plant, delivered the claims to the state unemployment office, picked up the benefit checks, and distributed them to workers at the headquarters plant. (This was not done at the Oregon and Alabama facilities where fewer employees were involved.) This procedure facilitated processing the claims and eliminated the need for employees to appear at the state unemployment office.

However, in 1979, the state unemployment insurance office required T-J employees to report to the MESC office to file papers and to pick up their checks. The unemployment insurance office changed the earlier procedure because of the opportunities it provided for fraud.

Operation

The steps followed by T-J as it considered, implemented, and reevaluated the program were as follows:

1. Determined the extent of workforce reduction required in terms of both decreased workload and decreased business income, and the cost savings to be achieved by adopting the program among various numbers of employees; also, estimated the length of time the reduced level of operations might be necessary. (For example, they initially predicted a 4-month program, but by the start of the third cycle they anticipated that the period would be shorter and, accordingly, began planning for such a change.)

2. Set up a rotation cycle and established criteria for participation. (According to Personnel Manager Robert V. Lieblein, an important aspect of rotation layoff is the selection of workers and assignments into groups. Each group must include workers who possess the range of skills required to perform and complete a production function. Another criteria used is seniority.)

3. Determined the unemployment insurance requirements and examined the feasibility of this approach with the state unemployment insurance office. (In 1979, T-J managers met with Michigan Employment Security Commission personnel to discuss any procedural or regulatory changes since the 1975 program.)

4. Informed employees about the program, discussed MESC rules, aided employees in completing required forms, and advised participants of their schedules. (T-J management sent news to all shop supervisors on rotation layoff, setting forth the rotation schedule.)

5. Continued to communicate with employees about the program. (When management thought the program might have to be extended or expanded, employees were informed and questioned about their preferences.)

6. Determined whether company objectives were met and whether workers were satisfied with the arrangement. (There is general agreement that the program helped retain skilled employees and provided T-J flexibility to increase its workforce quickly. As evidenced by the 1979 preference poll, employees were well satisfied with the program.)

Effect on Employees

In both 1975 and 1979, worker response to this approach was positive. The feeling was that T-J "demonstrated concern for the employee in hard times." Informal comments as well as responses to the 1977 opinion poll and the 1979 survey question underscored this response. However, in 1979, production workers complained that nonproduction personnel were exempt.

In July 1980, T-J implemented a 1 in 5 rotation layoff for 60 of its salaried employees, reflecting a decrease in sales and earnings. Only supervisors and the Engineering Department were exempted. The Engineering Department was only temporarily exempted until the unusually high work backlog could be reduced.

Employees retained their full employment status, with no loss in position or seniority. Basic pay rates were maintained. Participating employees could plan for their time off because of the predetermined and published schedule.

In Michigan and Alabama, where there is no waiting period for unemployment benefits, employee income was not interrupted. In 1975 and 1979, employees at the Oregon facility had a 1-week waiting period for the first cycle of the program.

The average net income loss per employee for one rotation cycle during 1979 was $140, or about $35 per week, according to Lieblein; over the entire 16-week program period, each participating employee lost an average total of $560. This management computation didn't take into account savings on such work-related expenses as transportation, meals, and child care.

Fringe benefits for participants, including medical and life insurance and paid holidays remained fully active. (This is in contrast to a complete layoff program wherein all employee benefits except group life and health insurance cease.)

As both the hourly 1979 rotation layoffs and salaried 1980 rotation layoffs were in the second half of their respective years, T-J required participating employees to cancel remaining vacation plans. Unused vacation was charged to each person during the layoff week, permissible under Michigan's unemployment insurance provisions. This continued during each rotation cycle, until the employee had used all vacation credits. Management felt this was necessary in order to have an adequate workforce available when business improved. Should the rotation program be stopped before all vacation time was used, employees would be able to use the remaining time any way they wished. If a rotation program were to be implemented before the beginning of the "vacation season," T-J would not require employees to use their vacation during layoff periods as that would create "undue hardships and would not be demanded by business necessity," observes Lieblein.

Effect on Company

Management met its objective of reducing payroll, and other objectives as well:

- Retaining machinists and other skilled workers;
- Avoiding rehiring and retraining employees;
- Maintaining high employee morale;
- Providing for production flexibility.

Lieblein stated that rotation layoff enables the company to respond immediately to a temporary or permanent increase in production scheduling demands. This flexibility was demonstrated at T-J during the rotation layoff period which began in October 1979. When an influx of orders was received, the fourth rotation cycle was postponed and finally cancelled.

Layoff rotation was flexible enough to use in conjunction with other normal operating activities such as holiday shutdowns.

Lieblein stressed that "rotation layoff is ideally suited to dealing with a temporary downturn. It is not the only management tool for responding to downturns, but offers so many advantages, both to the organization and to the employee, that it should be seriously considered as an alternative to traditional layoffs. Whatever the administrative effort may be, a rotation layoff program will pay off in terms of skills retention, production flexibility, and employee loyalty and goodwill.''

ROTATION LAYOFF
WITH SUPPLEMENTAL
UNEMPLOYMENT BENEFITS

Firestone Tire & Rubber Company
International Union of the United Rubber, Cork,
Linoleum and Plastic Workers of America,
AFL-CIO, CLC

The first master agreement between Firestone Tire and Rubber Company and the United Rubber Workers (URW) in the 1940s contained a work sharing provision. When production demand declined, all production workers were required to work a reduced week with reduced pay for up to eight consecutive weeks before layoff procedures were invoked. Impetus for this arrangement came from management's concern about maintaining productivity and retaining skilled workers. Then as now, when layoff occurred, seniority or "bumping rights" were invoked, causing numerous transfers and reassignments within the plant. Workers had to become acquainted with their new work tasks, equipment, and materials. Usually, productivity decreased during this shakedown period. Further, a percentage of laid off workers did not return when the company issued a recall, which led to increased company costs for hiring and training replacements.

Under the original work sharing arrangement, URW's senior members as well as other workers lost income. Protected against layoffs, these senior workers preferred layoffs to noncompensated work sharing schedules.

Over the years, contracts have retained the work sharing provision but have provided for partial compensation for lost earnings due to work reductions. And, as partial compensation benefits improved, work sharing became more popular among senior employees. Some senior workers now prefer work sharing to working full time during a layoff.

The Supplemental Unemployment Benefit Agreement was first negotiated in 1956 for layoff and later expanded to provide for short workweek benefits. Employees meeting the eligibility requirements for a short workweek benefit can receive 80 percent of their average hourly earnings lost for those hours not made available during the regular workweek.

In the event of layoff, benefits are provided according to a complex arrangement tied to State Unemployment Insurance Benefits and Company Supplemental Unemployment Benefits (SUB). Eligible workers receive 80 percent of their Weekly Straight Time Pay. Employees are obligated to apply for any state benefits for which they are eligible; the SUB Fund then adds to the state benefit the amount necessary to equal the 80 percent benefit. To be eligible for a regular benefit, an employee must receive a state benefit. However, if employees have exhausted their state system benefits but are otherwise eligible for SUB, the full 80 percent benefit is paid from the SUB Fund.

The collective bargaining agreement provides that the company can invoke either work sharing or layoff provisions during a production slowdown. Invariably, Firestone selects work sharing when production cutbacks are expected to be short term. Due to production requirements, Firestone's work sharing schedule is limited to shutting down entire plants or departments within a plant for one or two weeks, then returning to a normal work schedule for a week or two. If necessary, the company repeats the one or two week closedown.

The current contract limits work sharing to a reduction of no more than 48 hours over two consecutive weeks or during a 6-week period, as work sharing is less attractive than layoffs to both the company and senior employees after an extended period of time. The costs of fringe benefits and supervisory and clerical support are borne by Firestone under work sharing.

For workers, losses sustained under work sharing become burdensome after a while. The 17,500 URW hourly workers at the 12 Firestone plants average $10 an hour. Under work sharing, they lose 5 percent to 10 percent of their weekly wage (or $20 to $40). Worker anxiety increases when extensive work sharing and layoffs deplete the SUB Fund, endangering their 80 percent guarantee. As the fund nears depletion, senior workers demand layoffs to enable them to return to full-time work status.

In 1980, business conditions in the tire manufacturing industry were in a volatile state: *i.e.,* increased fuel costs led to less auto driving and reduced demand for tires; foreign cars imported with their own tires also reduced demand; market changes, such as increasing popularity of smaller and lighter cars, required the design of new types of tires. Firestone's business forecasts had been more optimistic than actual demand.

At the beginning of the year, Firestone had to reassess demand realities against plant capacity. While the study was being conducted, the company invoked work sharing extensively. At the end of the evaluation, Firestone was better able to make long term decisions on plant closings and layoffs.

Firestone officials consider work sharing an effective mechanism for minimizing disruptions for both workers and the company over the short term.

Shared Work Unemployment Compensation: Administration

The California Employment Development Department (EDD), which is responsible for operating the SWUC program in California, has tried to keep the administrative procedures simple to encourage participation and minimize program "red tape." A complete description of the SWUC program is included as an Appendix to the book.

To be approved, an employer plan must satisfy the following requirements:

- The reduction in wages paid and hours worked must be at least 10 percent in the affected work unit or units (work units are defined by the employer);
- If a collective bargaining agreement is in effect, the bargaining agent must agree to the plan in writing;
- The plan must identify all employees participating in the program and the reductions in each one's total wages and hours worked.

Once the EDD has approved the application (Exhibit A represents the UI form developed by EDD for the SWUC program), the employer must provide participating employees with a weekly statement of reduction in hours and wages which the workers use to claim their benefits.

Employers are charged for benefits in the same way they are charged for regular unemployment insurance benefits. However, participating employers whose recent use of unemployment insurance benefits exceeds their contribution to the fund (negative reserve accounts) are required to pay additional unemployment insurance taxes ranging from .5 to .3 percent on the first $6,000 of an employee's wage.

Employees must serve a 1-week noncompensated waiting period. After the initial claim, which employees must file personally, workers receive their unemployment checks directly from the state through the mail. Under the SWUC program, participants are not required to conduct a job search. Participating employees can only collect partial benefits up to 20 weeks during a 52-week period.

Exhibit A

WORK SHARING UNEMPLOYMENT INSURANCE BENEFIT PLAN

_____ hereby seeks approval of
(Name of Employer)

the following work or job sharing plan pursuant to Unemployment Insurance Code Section 1279.5.

1. Total number of employees in work force: _____

2. Total number of employees who would have been laid off if the Work Share Program had not been available: _____

Affected Work Unit Designation (Such as clerical, production, assembly)	Number of Employees in Unit	Number of Employees Sharing Work*
_____	_____	_____
_____	_____	_____
_____	_____	_____
_____	_____	_____
_____	_____	_____
TOTAL	_____	_____

3. Type of Business:_____

4. Reason for Work Reduction:_____

5. Expected Number of Weeks of Reduced Work:_____

6. Employer Account Number: _____

7. Full Company Name:_____

8. Company Doing Business As (DBA):_____

9. Address: _____
                  (P.O. Box or Street Address)

_____
(City)   (State)   (Zip Code)

10. Telephone Number: (_____)_____
                  (Area Code)

_____
                                        Signature of Employer

*NOTE: All employees who will be sharing work should be listed on the attached continuation sheet.

State of California Employment Development Department
DE 8686 Rev. 3 (11-79)

Full Employer Name:_____

Account Number:_____

Employees Sharing Work

	Name	SSA #	Percent of hours and wage reduction
1.			
2.			
3.			
4.			
5.			
6.			
7.			
8.			
9.			
10.			
11.			
12.			
13.			
14.			
15.			
16.			
17.			
18.			
19.			
20.			
21.			
22.			

SHARED WORK UNEMPLOYMENT COMPENSATION

Vendo Company

Founded in 1937, Vendo Company manufactures vending machines for hot and cold beverages. (Worldwide sales and marketing activities are directed from headquarters in Kansas.) Vendo's Pinedale, California plant employs 103 office workers and 441 hourly paid production workers. Of those 544, 25 percent are from minority groups and 15 percent are female. Wages range between $4.15 and $8.60 an hour, with an average of $5.75 per hour. Workers are represented by Local 653 of the International Machinists Union (IAM).

Decisionmaking

At the Pinedale plant, vending machine production is a proprietary line in which sales can be forecast; generally, summer is a busy season followed by a slowdown in the fall. During summer 1979, sales were lower than forecast, and a severe layoff of 75 to 80 workers seemed inevitable.

Previous layoffs had been costly to the company; a total of 50 percent of its most skilled workers had found jobs elsewhere. When demand increased, the expense of hiring and training replacements (some of whom didn't work out) was great. Further, Vendo received a higher unemployment experience rating, which meant an increased company contribution to the unemployment insurance system. Therefore, Personnel Manager Robert Berry explored California's Shared Work Unemployment Compensation (SWUC) program, which he had read about in a publication of the California Manufacturers Association. He met with representatives from the regional unemployment insurance office to get more information on program administration and impact on employees' earnings.

Berry estimated that a 20 percent reduction in work hours—from 40 hours to 32 hours a week—for the 4 months remaining in the year would enable the company to avoid a layoff. Because the company had worked at stabilizing its workforce since 1975, it now had a positive experience rating with the state unemployment insurance system, and Berry calculated that SWUC would draw less on unemployment funds than would layoffs, thus making it less expensive.

Satisfied with the approach, Berry presented the idea to top management at Vendo, who agreed that SWUC met company objectives of retaining skilled workers and stabilizing the workforce. Berry was directed to consult with union leaders.

Since 1975, management and labor had worked together to solve operational problems before they reached grievance level. (One solution to the normal fall slowdown had been to hire students during the summer to meet higher production demands, then to divide the decreased workload among permanent employees when the students returned to school in the fall.)

The union already knew about the unusually large drop in sales when Berry spoke to elected union business representative Gene Mills about the SWUC program as a possible alternative to layoff. SWUC is permitted under the temporary layoff provision in the union's contract with Vendo.

After sounding out the 14 shop stewards at Pinedale, who, in turn, discussed the program and its effect on earnings with plant workers, Mills concluded that workers did not want a layoff and the company should apply for the SWUC program. Among the reasons cited were:

- The union understood that the production decrease was a legitimate response to market conditions and that layoffs were likely.
- The union felt SWUC was the best alternative to protect its members. The most senior members in the union—about 40 percent of workers in the production area have 10 years of seniority, and a majority of women in the production area have 20 or more years of seniority—had been laid off in the past and understood the emotional and financial difficulties associated with layoffs. They were willing to help out the junior workers for a short period.
- Under SWUC, workers would receive 90 to 95 percent of their wages. In addition, they would continue to receive fringe benefits they would have lost had they been laid off.

The plan also would give workers their normal 40-hour workweek wages during the two holiday weeks of the program (September 2 and November 19) and their usual 2-week, fully paid vacation when the plant closed as usual during the last two weeks of August. In addition, there was no loss in membership dues to the union.

- Labor and management agreed that the measure was temporary.
- Management guaranteed that there would be no speed up in production.

Participation

Between July 16 and December 21, 1979, a total of 253 workers participated in the SWUC plan. The program affected departments most directly related to the vending line flow operations. All employees in five departments and some employees in three other departments participated. Not involved were departments already behind schedule or involved in operations whose business had increased.

Through normal attrition during the 5-month period, Vendo reduced its total workforce from 678 to 544 without a layoff. Only two of those who left cited the SWUC program as the reason for their departure.

Because of the substantial number of employees who would have been laid off had the SWUC program not been available, employees with four or five years of seniority might have been affected.

Program Administration

As soon as the company was certified to participate in the SWUC program, Vendo provided paid time off to participating employees to meet with representatives from the state unemployment insurance office who came to the plant to help workers file their initial claims. In succeeding weeks, the company facilitated processing the forms by providing employees with computer printouts of the claims form already indicating workers' earnings and worktime reduction for the previous week. Employees validated the information, signed the forms, and returned them to the personnel department for batch mailing to the unemployment insurance office. Berry said that the initial administrative activities required extra staff time but, once the process was computerized, the workload was minimal.

Employees did not have to go to the unemployment insurance office at any time. One problem for workers was a lapse time of about six weeks between the first claim and the receipt of the payment. Subsequent payments were made on schedule.

Employer Costs/Benefits

The company continued to pay employee fringe benefits during participation in SWUC. Estimated at $100 per month per employee, benefits included health insurance, dental plan, pension fund, vacation, and 10 paid holidays annually. Under the union's agreement with Vendo, the contribution to the pension plan could have been prorated, but Vendo decided not to elect that option.

Extra administrative costs were incurred in processing the SWUC forms, but based on past experience of having to replace skilled workers after a layoff, management believes that retention of the skilled workers more than offset these administrative costs.

An unanticipated positive outcome of the program was a drop in absenteeism, from 5 percent to 2.5 percent. One explanation is that workers took care of personal business, such as doctor's appointments, on their extra day off. Another explanation lies in the choice of Monday, traditionally a high absence day, as the "day off."

Another positive effect of the program, Berry observes, was the opportunity it provided supervisors and foremen not participating in SWUC to catch up on their paper work; in addition, many were able to attend training courses on safety and human relations, which production schedules had prevented in the past.

Employee Costs

Unemployment insurance benefits for Vendo employees were based on the highest earnings during the applicable quarters in 1978-1979. Since these benefits were nontaxable* and since the

*UI benefits are taxable under federal law to the extent that an individual's earned income exceeds $20,000.

unpaid period was small in relation to the paid period, the net difference in pay between the 40-hour and the 32-hour weeks was small. Also minimizing the difference in employees' earnings was the general hourly pay increase of $.29 to $.32 for those at the top of their rate and the scheduled quarterly increases of $.10 per hour for those not at the top of their rate, both effective two weeks after the SWUC program began.

The combination of four days' wages plus partial unemployment compensation for one day off and the scheduled wage increase resulted in most employees receiving almost the same take-home pay as before the temporary layoff. This lessened resistance to the work sharing plan.

The following table illustrates the difference between the wages for a normal 40-hour workweek and a 32-hour workweek under the SWUC arrangement.

Weekly Earnings & Unemployment Compensation for a Single Person
Claiming One Exemption and a Married Person Claiming Two Exemptions
(Other exemption schedules will vary slightly)

Single—One exemption

Rate	Hours	Gross	FICA	SDI	Federal	State	Net Pay
$4.95	40	$198.00	$12.13	$1.98	$27.00	$5.20	$151.69
4.95	32	158.40	9.71	1.58	18.60	3.00	125.51
						Difference	$ 26.18
						UI Benefit	17.00
						Net Difference	$ 9.18
5.07	40	202.80	12.43	2.03	29.10	5.60	$153.64
5.07	32	162.24	9.95	1.62	20.70	3.20	126.77
						Difference	26.87
						UI Benefit	17.40
						Net Difference	$ 9.47
5.60	40	224.00	13.73	2.24	33.80	6.90	$167.33
5.60	32	179.20	10.98	1.79	22.80	4.00	139.63
						Difference	27.70
						UI Benefit	18.80
						Net Difference	$ 8.90

Married—Two exemptions

Rate	Hours	Gross	FICA	SDI	Federal	State	Net Pay
$4.95	40	$198.00	$12.13	$1.98	$17.40	$1.40	$165.09
4.95	32	158.40	9.71	1.58	10.60	-0-	136.51
						Difference	28.58
						UI Benefit	17.00
						Net Difference	$ 11.58
5.07	40	202.80	12.43	2.03	19.20	1.80	167.34
5.07	32	162.24	9.95	1.62	12.10	-0-	138.57
						Difference	28.77
						UI Benefit	17.40
						Net Difference	$ 11.37
5.60	40	224.00	13.73	2.24	22.80	2.30	182.83
5.60	32	179.20	10.98	1.79	13.80	-0-	152.63
						Difference	30.20
						UI Benefit	18.80
						Net Difference	$ 11.40

Conclusion

In a letter to the California Employment Development Department to advise that Vendo was discontinuing the work sharing program, Berry wrote: "The program enabled us to avoid a major layoff and retain our trained work force. . . . We are well pleased with the program. It served a useful purpose during a difficult adjustment for us."

Labor and management agree that the SWUC program achieved the stated goals. Additionally, it had a positive effect on worker morale. Under similar circumstances, they would participate again.

SHARED WORK
UNEMPLOYMENT COMPENSATION

Duncan Enterprises

Duncan Enterprises is a Fresno-based hobby ceramics supplies manufacturer. Established by the Duncans in 1946, it has remained a family-owned business. It is unionized by the Laborers' International Union of North America. Average wages are $5.50 per hour. Approximately 70 percent of its workforce of 333 is male. In recent years, Duncan has given more emphasis to hiring females for production line jobs; currently, most female employees are office workers.

Duncan normally has a seasonal downturn in new orders during the winter months. Though temporary, these downturns have resulted in layoffs of skilled and semi-skilled manufacturing personnel.

Because of the company philosophy of taking care of its workers, management was receptive to different approaches to dealing with decreased personnel needs with a minimum upheaval for its employees.

Decisionmaking

After reading an article in the October 1979 *Business Week* that described California's Shared Work Unemployment Compensation (SWUC) program, Vice President of Manufacturing Lee Sneller suggested the program as a potentially beneficial tool during Duncan's imminent downturn period.

Employee Relations Manager William Bowen thought that SWUC could help in several ways:

- Enhance worker morale. Despite the seasonal layoffs, the organizational climate had been good; management wanted to maintain that atmosphere.
- Strengthen the employees' belief in management's commitment to job security and encourage trust between labor and management.

- Promote work group equity by retaining "junior" employees. Employees who had been hired during the past few months would have lost their jobs had a layoff been called.
- Reduce costs for hiring and training. In earlier layoffs, Duncan had lost some skilled and semi-skilled workers, which resulted in additional recruitment and training expenses.

Bowen explored the feasibility of adopting the SWUC program at Duncan by meeting with Fresno Regional Unemployment Insurance Office representatives. Since he knew the Personnel Manager of a participating California firm mentioned in the *Business Week* article, Robert Berry, he contacted Berry at Vendo Corporation to learn firsthand about the benefits and problems of the shared work program. Vendo's positive experience with shared work was a major factor in persuading Duncan to participate in the program.

As part of the development plan, Bowen and Sneller consulted with the business representative of Local 294, the Laborers' International Union of North America. Union representatives and stewards discussed the potential advantages and disadvantages of the shared work unemployment compensation plan and they gave their support for the program.

Program

Management had determined that a 20 percent reduction in work hours would be sufficient to avoid a layoff. During the 5-week program period (December 10, 1979 through January 14, 1980), participants worked four days, Tuesday through Friday, and collected unemployment insurance for Mondays. (Management selected Monday as the day off as research had shown that accident rates are higher on Monday than on other workdays.)

Duncan distributed a memorandum to bargaining unit employees describing the operation of the shared work unemployment program. The memo also stressed management's reasons for implementation, namely, to accomplish a short term cutback in manufacturing employees "with a minimal burden to our valued employees." (See Exhibit A.)

Managers and foremen attended briefings on the program's operations; in turn, they held informal meetings with employees

Exhibit A

INTER-OFFICE CORRESPONDENCE

To: .   Bargaining Unit Employees   Date: November 27, 1979

Copies To: See distribution

From: Lee J. Sneller
Vice President, Mfg.

Subject: Work Sharing Program

Due to the normal, seasonal downturn in new orders, Duncan's unfortunately must make a short-term cutback in Manufacturing. To accomplish this with a minimal burden to our valued employees, Duncan's and your union representatives have agreed to participate in the Work Sharing Program offered through the State of California Department of Employment. This outstanding new program will allow Duncan employees to receive approximately 90% of their normal pay yet actually work only four days a week.

Effective Monday, December 10, 1979 all manufacturing departments, except Maintenance, will go on a four-day (32-hour) work week of Tuesday through Friday. Through the Work Sharing Program, each affected employee will receive unemployment benefits for the fifth day from the Duncan-paid state unemployment insurance account. Typically, these benefits will pay the approximate equivalent of four hours' wages. Thus, in effect, you will receive (36) hours of total pay for only working (32) hours.

The Department of Employment requires that an employee must have served a one-week waiting period without benefits in order to be eligible for unemployment benefits. For this program, December 10th (Monday) will serve that requirement; thus, benefits will start on December 17th and December

10th will be an unpaid day (unless you have already served the waiting period in the past year).

Because December 10th serves as the waiting period, Duncan Bargaining Unit employees who are laid off for the three days over the Christmas holidays (December 26, 27, & 28) will be eligible to receive unemployment benefits for that period if they so desire. An employee who elects to take accrued vacation for the three days is not eligible for unemployment benefits for that period. Unemployment benefits will typically amount to about 40% of regular pay if you have been employed at Duncan's for a year or more.

Duncan has made arrangements with the Department of Employment to have all the proper forms filled out ahead of time so that it will not be necessary for Duncan employees to go downtown to the Department offices. Each employee will be required to sign the forms before becoming eligible for unemployment benefits. Your supervisor will hand out the forms at the appropriate time for your signature.

A decision will be made on each Thursday to determine if it is necessary for any particular department to work a full five days the following week. If such work is made available, each affected employee is required to work (by California Department of Employment rules).

We anticipate this change in the work week to last approximately two to three months. Duncan will make every effort to secure sufficient orders to allow us to return to a five-day week as soon as possible.

to answer further questions. A special effort was made to encourage the participation of senior workers.

Participation

A total of 137 employees participated in the SWUC program. Of these, 128 were hourly-paid production workers (all union members); 9 other participants were nonunion, salaried, quality control technicians.

Duncan employees—including its senior workers—were willing to participate for a number of reasons:

- There had been previous cyclical downturns, and employees were convinced that this work sharing program would be temporary.
- Workers sympathized with junior employees who would be laid off during the Christmas season if the program measures were not implemented.
- They would continue to receive about 90 percent of their wages with the unemployment compensation.
- Full fringe benefit coverage, including health, life and dental insurance, and employer pension contributions, would be maintained.
- Senior workers were willing to exchange small reductions in pay for leisure time during the holiday season.

Evaluation

Costs. Duncan had a positive reserve account with the unemployment insurance fund and does not expect the SWUC program to increase their contribution rating.

The company did not perform a rigorous cost-benefit analysis of the SWUC program. Management believes that the positive response to SWUC, translated into retention of skilled workers and good will between employees and management, have more than offset fringe benefit and administrative costs associated with the program.

Training. According to Bowen, the free Mondays provided time for supervisory training of foremen.

Administration. Processing the weekly certification forms for SWUC was burdensome. Manufacturing Division foremen and the Employee Relations Department spent several hours each week on administrative paperwork, entering the earnings and worktime reductions for the previous week on 137 forms and then batch-mailing them to the unemployment insurance office.

Employee Morale. Overall, employees responded positively to the shared work approach. Some workers resented receiving lower unemployment compensation than co-workers earning the same hourly wage, despite an explanation for the differences from unemployment insurance representatives during their visit to Duncan to register program participants. Under the unemployment insurance system, compensation is based on previous quarters of earnings; hence, even if workers had the same earnings at the time they registered, calculations were based on their earlier, lower earnings.

Duncan's management supports SWUC as a new approach that alleviates for employer and employee the stresses of a layoff caused by a cyclical downturn. Benefits outweigh negative aspects, according to Bowen, but the administrative paperwork is one part of the program that needs streamlining.

SHARED WORK UNEMPLOYMENT COMPENSATION

Mary Jane Company

The Mary Jane Company of North Hollywood, California, is a closely-held corporation that produces maternity undergarments. More than 85 percent of the 300 office and manufacturing workers are women. Approximately 70 percent of the workforce is Spanish-speaking. Production workers include assemblers, seamstresses, cutters, utility workers, and bundlers. Through piece work incentives, a skilled worker can increase the base hourly wage of $3.40 to between $6.50 and $8.00.

Decisionmaking

Retention of skilled workers was the primary reason the Mary Jane Company participated in California's Shared Work Unemployment Compensation (SWUC) program, according to Personnel Administrator Esther Wontka. In 1979, the company faced the first threat of a layoff in its 34-year history. Inventory revealed an overstock of a number of clothing items. Managers believed that the sales forecast for the remainder of the year did not justify current production rates. Management was concerned that they might have to lay off workers and, in the process, might lose the most skilled employees.

Just as layoffs were being considered, Mary Jane received a leaflet from the local unemployment insurance office announcing a seminar on SWUC, sponsored by the State Economic Development Department. Wontka attended and later presented information on the objectives and operation of SWUC to top management at the company. With their approval, Wontka explored the feasibility of implementing a SWUC program at Mary Jane.

Wontka recommended a 20 percent reduction in work hours—that is, one day off each week—until the inventory reached acceptable levels. The flexibility of the California program, she believed, would enable Mary Jane to return to normal, full-time operations before company workers reached the maximum number of weeks for unemployment insurance. Wontka had estimated that 184 workers would have to be laid off for four to six weeks if the company did not participate in SWUC.

Program

Between September 3, 1979, and January 5, 1980, 180 female and 5 male production workers at Mary Jane participated in the SWUC program. Participating employees worked regular schedules Monday through Thursday and were off on Fridays. Partial compensation for the reduced salary came from state unemployment insurance.

Initially, representatives of the local unemployment insurance office came to Mary Jane to register work sharing personnel and facilitate the processing of forms. In subsequent weeks, Mary Jane's Personnel Department prepared the weekly certification forms for employees and batch-mailed them to the local unemployment insurance office.

Mary Jane continued to pay the benefits normally received by hourly and salaried workers. For example, the company paid health insurance and a contribution to the Employee Stock Ownership Plan to its hourly workers. However, vacation accrual, which at Mary Jane is based on a percentage of annual earnings, was affected by the reduced hours.

Effect on Employees

Employees at Mary Jane view the program favorably, as it provided:

- Job retention. A combination of nonfluency in English by many of the Spanish-speaking production workers and lack of readily transferable skills presented barriers to employment elsewhere.

- Ease in commuting. A number of the female workers commuted to their jobs with their husbands, employed in nearby firms. Other manufacturing companies likely to hire laid-off Mary Jane production workers were located in a different area of Los Angeles which was not readily accessible by public transportation.

- Economic security. Most Mary Jane employees indicated that they had to work; layoffs would have created financial strains on their families. Although they preferred full-time work, they agreed that work sharing was useful as a short term method to reduce the economic impact of a production slowdown as they were aware of their difficulties in finding other employment.

- Continued fringe benefits.

Effect on Management

Prior to adoption of the program, management had been concerned principally about administrative time and cost, the impact of the program on the unemployment insurance contribution rate (that is, experience rating), and the retention of skilled workers.

- Two aspects of program administration were found to be burdensome. Personnel files at Mary Jane are not computerized, and completion of the weekly certification forms for each employee required considerable staff time. Additionally, material about the program from the unemployment insurance office was printed only in English, whereas Mary Jane's workforce is predominantly Spanish-speaking with only a rudimentary knowledge of English. To ensure that employees understood the reasons for the program and the forms they needed to sign, supervisors held meetings with line employees.

- Management had been concerned that if Mary Jane's unemployment insurance contribution rate increased, some of the other program benefits might be offset. However, calculations by the local unemployment insurance office indicated that participation in SWUC would not adversely affect Mary Jane's experience rating or its positive reserve account with the unemployment insurance fund.

- Had it become necessary to resort to layoffs, some of its skilled workers would have found jobs elsewhere. Under the program, management averted this loss.

Another benefit to the company was the opportunity work sharing provided for production supervisors to organize their work and catch up on backlog paperwork on free Fridays.

Overall, Mary Jane's management was pleased with the results of the program. Despite the administrative inconveniences noted earlier, shared work was, according to Wontka, an effective tool for managing a short economic downturn.

2
PERMANENT REDUCTION
IN WORK HOURS

Three reduced work scheduling arrangements—shorter workweeks without reductions in pay, part time (including job sharing), and extended vacations and/or holidays—belong in the category of permanent reduction in work hours.

Typically, these arrangements are initiated in response to an employee desire for reduced work hours and/or longer periods of leisure. Some are negotiated by unions in collective bargaining agreements. Others are set up by management to accommodate individual employee requests or to recruit potential employees. The reduction schedule depends on employer objectives, production demands, labor goals, and employee preferences. Methods include cutbacks in workdays, workweeks, or workyears.

Permanently reduced work hour arrangements are institutionalized in personnel policies and collective bargaining agreements. These are distinguished from temporary work hour reductions that are of limited duration and initiated in response to economic downturns (as described in chapter 1).

Shorter Workweeks

Shorter workweeks are permanent reductions in the weekly work hours without reduction in pay.

The 68-hour workweek of 1860 has been reduced over the years to the current 40-hour workweek. Substantial reductions occurred between 1901 and 1948, when the workweek fell from 58.4 hours a week to 42.0. The Fair Labor Standards Act (FLSA), passed in 1938, reduced the standard workweek from 48 to 40 hours and created a premium for overtime. This 40-hour workweek has persisted in most industries since the 1930s. In some industries (service, wholesale, and retail trade, for example) the decline in the mean number of hours worked during a workweek has resulted principally from the entrance of large numbers of part-time workers.

While demands for reduced worktime have played a central role in the American labor movement, other issues gained precedence following World War II, according to Sar A. Levitan and Richard S. Belous.[1] These include wage increases, fringe benefits, and occupational health and safety. Labor's collective bargaining emphasis in reduced worktime shifted from reduced workweeks to extended holidays, vacations, personal days, and other paid leave gains for its members. Demographic, social, and economic changes during the last decade—the influx of women into the labor force, the reduced size of families, the increasing number of multiple earner households, and a growing demand for leisure—have refocused labor demands for shorter work hours.

Coming together under the banner of the "All Unions Committee," international unions, labor councils, and union locals organized during the mid-1970s to press for adoption of a 35-hour standard workweek. The Committee objectives are to maintain job security and to reduce unemployment by creating additional job opportunities.

---

1. Sar A. Levitan and Richard S. Belous, *Shorter Hours, Shorter Weeks: Spreading the Work to Reduce Unemployment,* Baltimore: Johns Hopkins University Press, 1977.

Labor representatives are apprehensive that the overtime provision of FLSA of 1938, created to spur new employment, has ceased to be an effective incentive for new hires as the costs of hiring, training, and paying the fringe benefits of new workers have overtaken the cost of paying premium overtime rates.

In what he views as an effort to reduce joblessness without sacrificing productivity, Representative John Conyers (D-MI) introduced in the 95th Congress, and reintroduced in the 96th, legislation that would reduce the standard workweek from 40 to 35 hours over a 4-year period. His Fair Labor Standard Amendments (H.R. 1784) would also eliminate compulsory overtime, and raise the overtime rate from time-and-a-half to double time. Three days of hearings (October 23, 24, 25, 1979) were held before the House Labor Standards Subcommittee of the Education and Labor Committee, but no further action was taken. Rep. Conyers has reintroduced the bill in the 97th Congress.

Although labor has strongly supported the shorter workweek, it has generally opposed the compressed workweek, that is, arrangements allowing workers to accomplish full-time work in less than the standard 5-day week by extending the workday beyond eight hours. Nevertheless, the adoption by companies of the compressed workweek has contributed to a reduction in work hours. Following a rush in the early 1970s to adopt compressed workweeks—usually four 10-hour days as promoted by Riva Poor's book *4 Days, 40 Hours*[2]—and amid mixed reports of its effects, a number of companies grew concerned that a 10-hour day would cause fatigue or family problems for some employees. Some companies have chosen to reduce their normal workweek, for example, from 40 to 38 hours or from 37.5 to 36 hours.

---

2. Riva Poor, ed. *4 Days, 40 Hours: Reporting a Revolution in Work and Leisure,* Cambridge, MA: Bursk and Poor Publishing, 1970.

In some instances, the total annual work hours were approximately equal to those before adoption of the compressed workweek by adjusting holidays. Either way, employees had substantially more days off a year, most resulting in 3-day weekends.

Part Time

Part-time work is a reduction in total work hours, accompanied by a reduction in salaries and, in some cases, by prorated fringe benefits.

Part-time employment is not a new work arrangement. It traditionally has been used by private and public employers—extensively in retail establishments and restaurants for example—to meet business needs such as increased or shifting workload demands. Part-time workers typically have been ineligible for fringe benefits and have been employed extensively in nonprofessional positions. Beyond the more conventional uses of part-time employees, some companies have developed innovative and creative part-time arrangements to meet varied employer and employee needs.

Retirees, for example, have been hired on a part-time basis with success. They not only are experienced workers, but often maintain flexible enough schedules to adapt to the changing needs of the organization. The company gains additional benefits when it rehires its own retirees by gaining workers already knowledgeable about company operations.

Part-year programs represent still another part-time approach. A summer-off option, for example, has appeal for parents with school-age children. These programs have been particularly useful in providing training to inexperienced or unskilled individuals who might not be able to work otherwise and may provide opportunities for participants to move into full-time positions when they so wish, if their job performance has been satisfactory.

In *permanent part-time* arrangements, employees voluntarily work substantially fewer hours or days than do full-time workers. The key difference between traditional part time and career-oriented part time is that these latter jobs were originally considered permanent, full-time positions. Permanent part-time work usually means opportunities for career advancement and eligibility for the same fringe benefits as full-time career employees, but generally with benefits prorated according to the number of hours worked. In recent years, permanent part-time positions have opened up for professional level employees.

One form of permanent part time that is gaining increasing attention is *job sharing*. According to Gretl Meier,[3] job sharing is a voluntary arrangement whereby two or more employees, each working less than full time, divide responsibilities and duties of one full-time position. (Other names for this arrangement are splitting, pairing, twinning, tandem, and split tour.)

Significantly, "permanent" is not necessarily permanent from the point of view of the individual, who may wish to work a reduced hour schedule at a reduced salary only during a particular life phase. Alan Cohen and Herb Gadon make an important distinction between the employee's view of part-time work and the organization's perspective. They note, "permanent part-time positions may indeed be more permanent in that they are available indefinitely regardless of the tenure of the jobholder."[4]

---

3. Gretl Meier, *Job Sharing: A New Pattern for Quality of Work and Life*, Kalamazoo, MI: W.E. Upjohn Institute for Employment Research, 1979.
4. Alan Cohen and Herman Gadon, *Alternative Work Schedules: Integrating Individual and Organizational Needs*, New York: Addison-Wesley Publishing Company, 1978.

Part-time arrangements vary. Employees may work just a few hours five days a week, full days a few days each week, or alternating weeks or months. Sometimes, arrangements are individually negotiated between the employer and employee; in other instances, broad programs are established to increase part-time employment.

Among the reasons given by organizations for starting permanent part-time programs are: to retain skilled employees, to meet affirmative action goals, to ease the transition from work to retirement, to reduce the workforce without laying off employees, to accommodate the needs of certain individuals, to increase job satisfaction, to improve efficiency, and to meet skill shortages.

The Equitable Life Assurance Society has provided employees with opportunities for a reduced workweek for many years. Recognizing that some people want less than full-time work and that some jobs warrant less than full-time assignment, Equitable allows employees to negotiate with managers to reduce their work schedules to at least one-half of the standard workweek of 36.25 hours.

Part-time workers at Equitable who are salaried and have been with the company for at least three years are designated "limited time" employees. These workers are eligible for the same program of insured benefits and time off as are full-time salaried employees, with the amount of benefits and leave prorated according to their schedule of hours and earnings. In 1980, approximately 196 employees were on "limited time." After a year with the company, workers who receive an hourly wage and work at least one-half of the regularly scheduled workweek are termed "modified limited-time" employees. These workers are eligible for a limited program of employee benefits. Approximately 600 employees now have "modified limited-time" status.

In 1972, when Micro Switch of Marlborough, Massachusetts, a small (233 employees) manufacturing division of Honeywell, experienced a shortage of reliable entry-level assemblers in its manufacturing departments, the company decided to appeal to people in the community who might wish to work four to six hours a day. The response was excellent, particularly from mothers of school-age children. These permanent part-time workers are not eligible for medical and dental benefits, but are offered all other fringe benefits on a prorated basis. Personnel Manager Louise I. Hale says the company views the part-time program as a way of fulfilling social responsibility, meeting the company's employment requirements, and improving productivity.

Legislative and Administrative Activities

Legislation establishing part-time career employment programs in federal agencies was approved during the 95th Congress, 2nd Session, having been introduced and considered by Congress in various forms since 1971. The prime sponsors of the legislation in their respective houses were former Senator Gaylord Nelson (D-WI), Senator Thomas Eagleton (D-MO), and Representative Patricia Schroeder (D-CO). Designed to ensure that part-time career opportunities exist as an employment option in the federal government at all grade levels, the Federal Employees Part-Time Career Employment Act became public law (PL 95-437) on October 10, 1978. The Office of Personnel Management (OPM) has jurisdiction over this matter.

Final regulations took into account recommendations by employee labor organizations and other groups; the regulations prohibit abolishment of occupational positions to make them available on a part-time basis and prevent full-time employees from being required to accept part-time work as a condition of employment.

Among its provisions, the law established, effective October 1980, a full-time equivalency personnel system for part-time employees which counts them in terms of hours worked rather than as position slots. A joint OPM/Office of Management and Budget administratively-initiated experiment was established between 1978 and 1979 to permit use of the full-time equivalency method for all employees in five selected federal agencies: the Veterans Administration, the Environmental Protection Agency, the Federal Trade Commission, the General Services Administration, and the Export-Import Bank.

To facilitate procedures for persons interested in part-time federal employment as well as to ease recruitment for agencies, a special Direct Hire program was established in July 1980. Selected federal agencies are now participating in a two-year experimental program to directly fill 300 professional and administrative career part-time positions in Washington, D.C. and selected areas around the country. Persons hired under the Direct Hire system are prohibited from moving to full-time work schedules until they have completed at least one year of part-time service.

In June 1980, oversight hearings to review the progress of agencies in expanding part-time employment were held by the Senate Committee on Governmental Affairs Subcommittees on Governmental Efficiency and the District of Columbia, and on Civil Service and General Services. Between Fall 1977 (when then President Carter directed agencies to expand permanent part time) and December 1980, the number of career part-time employees in the federal government increased by almost 30,000.

In addition to these bills and executive actions dealing with public sector employment, Representative Barber Conable (R-NY) introduced a measure into the 95th Congress which was designed to stimulate permanent part-time employment in the private sector. The bill would have provided tax credits to employers for a portion of the wages paid to certain part-time employees, with higher credits given for higher salaries. No action was taken on the measure by the House Ways and Means Committee.

During the past several years, there has been a substantial increase in implementation of permanent part-time programs by states. A recent survey of state agencies by the National Council for Alternative Work Patterns and the National Governors' Association reveals that thirty-four states allow permanent part-time employment in state agencies, and 19 have job sharing programs for their employees.[5] Some permanent part-time and job sharing programs are statewide; others are in selected agencies.

The Comprehensive Employment and Training Act (CETA) Amendments of 1978 require employment training services to include part-time and flexible work arrangements for CETA recipients unable to work full time. Further, the Department of Labor is directed to undertake research exploring the feasibility of reduced and flexible work hour arrangements in various settings.

Extended Holidays and Vacations

Substantial increases in holidays and vacations which extend employees' paid leave time are established through changes in personnel policies and collective bargaining agreements. These extensions are means of shortening working hours without reducing pay and in ways that still allow companies to meet production needs.

---

5. Marion C. Long and Susan W. Post, *State Alternative Work Schedule Manual* Washington: National Council for Alternative Work Patterns and National Governors' Association, 1981.

Generally, the extensions are part of an entire benefits package. In some instances, however, extended leave is offered as an incentive to stimulate productivity gains. For example, under a negotiated union agreement, some city employees in Hartford, Connecticut can earn one and one-half days of additional paid personal leave for each 3-month period of perfect attendance.

When labor pushed hard for more generous fringe benefit packages following World War II, it was interested in pursuing shorter workweeks, but dropped such demands before the hard bargaining began. With the recession and accompanying (and continuing) high unemployment, demands for reduced worktime again became a central bargaining issue as a way to increase employment opportunities. A number of these demands have been for extended paid time off rather than for reductions in the workweek. This approach is viewed by labor as an effective way to create jobs with minimal effect on job security and seniority of union members. Collectively bargained extended leaves additionally reflect the desire by some workers to take more of their total compensation package in the form of leisure.

SHORTER WORKWEEK

Medtronic, Inc.

Medtronic, Inc. is a bio-medical electronic equipment manufacturer, pioneering in the manufacture of Pacemakers. Annual sales total $283 million. Established in 1949, Medtronic, Inc. now has a workforce of 4,300 with 2,600 working at 11 locations in the Minneapolis, Minnesota area. Women comprise approximately 76 percent of the total workforce, but nearly 88 percent of production workers.

Decisionmaking

Impetus for a shortened workweek, according to management, came from a group of employees. For some years, they had asked management to consider changing the workweek during the summer so workers could leave early on Fridays. In the spring of 1971, having just gone through a period of rapid growth (annual gross sales had reached $35 million and the workforce had increased to 1,050), management decided to consider the employees' request. (At that time, females comprised 40 percent of the total workforce and 50 percent of manufacturing operations.)

A study group was formed to consider several 4-day workweek schedules, including:

- 4-day week, 10 hours per day
- 4-day week, 9 hours per day
- 4-day week, 8 hours per day
- 4.5-day week, 8.5 hours per day and 6 hours on Friday.

The group:

- Reviewed the literature on 4-day workweeks, including case studies of firms that had experimented with these schedules, and consulted with Riva Poor, author of the popular book *4 Days, 40 Hours;*
- Analyzed Medtronic's production and employee scheduling requirements (such as transportation and home arrangements);

- Studied federal and state laws and regulations relating to work hours (e.g., Fair Labor Standards, Walsh-Healey);
- Compared costs of alternatives to present scheduling; and
- Determined the impact on employee benefits.

The group concluded that Medtronic, Inc. could continue to meet product demand if the schedule were changed.

An Executive Planning Group reviewed the findings of the study and decided to reduce the workweek to 36 hours (four 9-hour days)—on a trial basis—with no reduction in pay and benefits. Each division was given two weeks to determine how the scheduling changes could be accomplished. The Executive Management Committee then worked out the minor problems that had been identified and the trial program began.

Program

A 3-month trial period began June 7, 1971. All employees except those in the International Division and in the field sales offices were eligible for the program. Most employees elected to work Monday through Thursday, but a sufficient number worked the Tuesday through Friday schedule to provide 5-day coverage.

While fringe benefits were maintained, management revised somewhat its policies on vacation accrual, holidays, overtime, and time off with and without pay to allow the equivalent benefits in the shortened workweek. Nonexempt workers' payday was changed from Friday to Thursday, when all workers were present. (Exhibits A-E describe some of the revised practices.)

Management analysis at the end of the 3-month trial revealed that company goals were being met: Medtronic had maintained or improved high standards of service to its customers, high standards of quality, production requirements, and coordination among departments. "In fact," reported Medtronic President Earl E. Bakken, "we have not only sustained overall productivity but have increased it in many areas."

The trial was then extended for another three months, to:

- Allow employees to evaluate the new schedule under a different set of conditions: the return of children to school, the

Exhibit A

INTER-OFFICE MEMO

TO: All Managers and Supervisors

FROM:

DATE: December 8, 1971

SUBJECT: Holidays and Absenteeism
             Under Reduced Workweek

HOLIDAYS

Due to our varying reduced workweek schedules it has become necessary to revise holiday scheduling so that each employee receives the proper amount of paid time off for holidays without changing the original policy intent, the following changes are being made:

> Employees scheduled for the 5 day, 40 hour week will receive nine (8 hour) paid holidays or a total of 72 hours.

> Employees scheduled on the 4 day, 36 hour reduced workweek will receive eight (9 hour) paid holidays or a total of 72 hours.

ABSENTEEISM

Each manager should continue to monitor employee time off, and employees scheduled on the reduced workweek should use their day off for personal business as well as doctor and dentist visits.

Your Human Resource Manager will be working with you to answer any questions or eliminate problems connected with the reduced workweek.

TAM/vlt
Attachments: I - 1971 Christmas Day and New Year's Day
             Holidays
             II - 1972 Scheduled Paid Holidays

July 4th Holiday

I. Work Schedule - 4-9 hour day

Mon. Tues. Wed. Thurs.

Holiday falls on:	Observed on:
Sunday	Monday

II. Work Schedule - 4-9 hour day

Tues. Wed. Thurs. Fri.

Holiday falls on:	Observed on:
Sunday	Tuesday

III. Work Schedule - 5-8 hour day

Mon. Tues. Wed. Thurs. Fri.

Holiday falls on:	Observed on:
Sunday	Monday

Since Holidays will be taken on different days based on work schedule, be sure that your coverage is adequate during these periods.

X = Schedule work days

☐ = Company observed holiday

				July			
4	5	6	7	8	9	10	
Sun.	Mon.	Tues.	Wed.	Thurs.	Fri.	Sat.	
	☒	X	X	X			4-9 hour day
		☒	X	X	X		4-9 hour day

Employees on a 40-32 hour scheduled alternating workweek, the following will apply.

				July			
4	5	6	7	8	9	10	
Sun.	Mon.	Tues.	Wed.	Thurs.	Fri.	Sat.	
	☒	X	X	X			4-8 hour day
	☒	X	X	X	X		5-8 hour day
		☒	X	X	X		4-8 hour day
	☒	X	X	X	X		5-8 hour day

Exhibit C

Banked Vacations

1. Banked vacation days will be converted to reduced workweek equivalents when days banked are in increments of five:

Example

Banked days	Weeks off (4 day 36)	Time off 40-32 scheduled alternating workweek
5	1	
10	2	40 hrs. week = 4 1/2 days
15	3	32 hrs. week = 4 days + 4 hours

2. For those days between 1 through 4 and 11 through 14, etc., banked vacation days will be converted at the rate of 7.2 hours per 8 hour banked vacation day.

Example

A Earned days off	B Conver. hours earned	C Time taken off	D Hrs. left to work in week	E Vacation hrs. used vs. credit	F Hours paid in week (B & D)
1	7.2	1/2 day = 4.5 hrs. 1 day = 9 hrs.	31.5 27	7.2-4.5 = 2.7 7.2-9 = (1.8)	36 + 2.7 34.2
2	14.4	1 1/2 days = 13.5 hrs.	22.5	14.4-13.5 = .9	36 + .9
3	21.6	2 days = 18 hrs.	18	21.6-18 = 3.6	36 + 3.6
4	28	3 days = 27 hrs.	9	28.8-27 = 1.8	36 + 1.8

Exhibit D

General Pay Practices

40 hour weekly salary will be paid for 36 hour workweek.

Regular hourly rate will be 40 hour weekly salary divided by 36 hours.

Example

40 hour workweek	36 hour workweek
$120.00 Salary	$120.00 salary
$3.00/hour	$3.334/hour
$4.50/hour O.T.	$5.001/hour O.T.

1½ times new regular hourly rate will be paid for all hours worked over 40 in a workweek.

2 times new regular hourly rate will be paid for Sundays worked, or for the 7th consecutive day, when worked, if normal workweek begins on a day other than Monday.

2 times new regular hourly rate for hours worked on a holiday plus holiday pay at new regular rate.

3 hours, 36 minutes minimum will be paid for those called back to work.

2nd & 3rd Shift Differential

Second shift employees will continue to be paid an additional 10¢/hour base pay differential.

Third shift employees will continue to be paid an additional 15¢/hour base pay differential.

NOTE: No change in present policy since shift differential is paid as an inconvenience premium for hours actually worked other than normal day schedule.

Additional Pay Practices for Employees on Fixed 36 Hour Workweek

Straight time at new regular rate will be paid for all hours over 36 and up to and including 40 hours.

Example

40 hour workweek	36 hour workweek
40 hours = $120.00	36 hours = $120.00
	37 hours + 3.334 = $123.334
	38 hours + 3.334 = $126.668
	39 hours + 3.334 = $130.002
	40 hours + 3.334 = $133.336

41 hours =
    40 hours @ 3.00 = $120.00
    + 1 hour @ 4.50 =   4.50
                Total $124.50

41 hours =
    40 hours @ 3.334 = $133.336
    + 1 hour @ 5.001 =   5.001
                Total $138.337

return to standard time, and the onset of winter; and
- Permit management to review performance over a longer time.

Evaluation of Trial Periods

Analysis showed that over the two trial periods (Exhibit F):

- Absenteeism dropped from a little over 5 percent to less than 4 percent;
- Turnover decreased from 13 percent to slightly more than 8 percent;
- Productivity increased (approximately 5 percent) or at least was maintained;
- Morale improved and employee commitment was strengthened;
- Recruitment became easier; and
- The company image was enhanced due to publicity about the program.

Employees viewed the program favorably. Among the benefits they perceived were: no loss of salary or fringe benefits; more time with family; savings in commuting expenses; more relaxing weekends; and pride in their company.

On the basis of these positive results, management elected to continue the reduced workweek on an indefinite trial basis, to be continued as long as aforementioned objectives were achieved.

Medtronic attributed the program's success in meeting organizational and employee needs to extensive research and planning, employee involvement, and continuing communication with all involved. Employees were advised of the company's policies, changing practices, and operational guidelines by letters and memos from Medtronic's President and articles in the company's newsletter and magazine.

Adapting to Change

In 1973, Medtronic began to receive purchase orders from the federal government exceeding $10,000; this brought the company under the jurisdiction of the Walsh-Healey Public Contract Act, which requires payment at time-and-a-half for hours worked in excess of 8 per day or 40 per week. A number of compliance alter-

Exhibit F

Reduced Workweek
Medtronic, Inc.

	Date	Productivity[1] Percent	Absenteeism[2] Percent
	April 1971	69	5.8
	May	67	5.0
(First trial)	June	74	3.3
	July	79	3.8
	August	79	3.3
(Second trial)	September	77	3.7
	October	74	4.7
	November	72	3.7

Fiscal year	Turnover Percent
April 30, 1968	19.0
April 30, 1969	15.9
April 30, 1970	14.9
April 30, 1971	13.0
June thru October 1971	8.2

1. Figures obtained from Rice Creek Productivity Report.
2. Figures obtained from Absenteeism Cost Analysis Report.

In general, since these trial periods, Medtronic, Inc. has been able to meet or exceed these standards. (Average absenteeism for last calendar year was 3.5 percent and turnover approximately 10.4 percent.)

natives were analyzed and Medtronic decided to pay the one hour of overtime for each of the four 9-hour days. The cost of compliance (payroll costs increased by 5.5 percent) was integrated into the annual salary increase program.

In 1977 it was determined that one of the objectives of the reduced workweek program, that of providing appropriate service and support to Medtronic's customers and sales force, was not being met. In order to ensure appropriate 5-day coverage, each division head was asked to examine the work schedules for all nonproduction personnel and to make adjustments as necessary. A number of alternative schedules were implemented, including a return to five 8-hour days. The production personnel, who have no interface with customers, remained on the reduced workweek. A few months later, due to inequities in work schedules across divisions and the resulting employee dissatisfaction, a uniform 36-hour workweek was reinstated. This workweek, termed "32-40," ensured 5-day coverage by alternating between four 8-hour days one week and five 8-hour days the next. Employees were given either Monday or Friday off on their short week. Under this arrangement, which has been very well received, employees still enjoy a 3-day weekend every other week, and effective 5-day coverage is provided.

SHORTER WORKWEEK

Ideal Industries

A manufacturer of electrical equipment for contractors and electricians, Ideal Industries has 650 employees. The company was founded in 1916 in Chicago by J. Walter Becker, who joined in partnership with his brother the following year and then moved in 1924 to Sycamore, Illinois where general offices have remained. The company incorporated in 1946.

As a family-owned company in a small community—Sycamore has a population of 9,000—Ideal's organizational climate is characterized by close personal relationships. The company's president meets with all employees at least four times a year to discuss business operations, problems, and possible changes. Ideal's Chairman of the Board often walks through the plant and offices to chat with employees about their jobs and families.

Management views Ideal as "progressive," according to Personnel Representative Beverly Rempfer. In a recent regional compensation survey, Ideal ranked in the top 10 percent of area firms. Rempfer attributes the company's low employee turnover rate to the quality of Ideal's plan, which includes company-paid medical and dental insurance, accident and disability coverage, life insurance, profit sharing and retirement plans, tuition reimbursement, a 4-day workweek, and flexitime.

In 1970, the Personnel Department began to explore the feasibility of adopting a compressed (4-day) workweek at Ideal. Such an arrangement was seen principally as a way to provide employees with more usable leisure time through a longer weekend, according to Ideal Treasurer William Awalt.

Investigation of the legal implications of extending the workday revealed that Ideal would be able to convert to this work schedule without legal problems. But a major consideration, one for which evidence was not as conclusive, was the potentially negative effect of a longer workday on employee morale, safety, and physical well-being: a 10-hour day might cause fatigue and make coordination with family activities more difficult. Because of these concerns, Awalt reports, Ideal shortened the workweek from 40 to 38 hours, thereby making a workday 9.5 hours. It was thought that the reduction might make the compressed schedule more appealing to employees and that the cost of the work hour reduction could be offset by shutting down the plant one additional day a week and by maintaining productivity.

Consistent with its tradition of keeping open channels of communication, management met with employees to explain why a compressed workweek was being considered and to determine employee reaction. When hourly and salaried employees reacted favorably, a 3-month trial period was initiated.

- The standard workweek was 9.5 hours a day, Monday through Thursday.
- Wages of hourly and salaried employees were recomputed to provide the same base amount under the 38-hour workweek as paid under the 40-hour week.
- Overtime was paid for any work beyond 9.5 hours a day or 38 hours a week.
- Holidays that fell on Friday were celebrated on Thursday.
- A skeleton crew was established to work Tuesdays through Fridays to provide services such as switchboard, shipping, receiving, and to cover the Customer Service Department.

At the end of the trial period, informal discussions with employees and supervisors were held. The overwhelmingly favorable response, coupled with a positive evaluation of the effects on company operations, led to the adoption of the 38-hour compressed workweek as a permanent arrangement at the Sycamore facility.

Only a few modifications have been made during the past 10 years. Since 1976, office employees have been able to work a flexitime schedule within the parameters of the 4-day/38-hour workweek. Further, during summers, at the request of production workers, the standard plant hours of 7:00 AM to 5:00 PM usually are changed to 6:30 AM to 4:30 PM.

Effect on Company

Although specific data are no longer available, the company's evaluation of the 3-month trial period concluded that there were substantial benefits in recruitment, employee morale, and absenteeism, and that productivity was maintained.

- Absenteeism. It was found that employees scheduled medical appointments and conducted personal business on Fridays. A reduction in short term absences resulted.
- Productivity. Initially, productivity increased under the compressed workweek schedule. When the schedule's novelty wore off, productivity returned to the previous level.
- Recruitment. Many new employees have commented that they applied to Ideal because they were attracted to the 4-day workweek.
- Morale. Employees view the schedule as a valued fringe benefit. They feel the 3-day weekend compensates for the longer workdays. When they do work an extra day overtime during periods of increased production, they still have a 2-day weekend.

Rempfer says it would be difficult to revert to a 5-day workweek at this point. "The long-lasting success of the arrangement," she observes, "can be attributed to our employees' enthusiasm."

SHORTER WORKWEEK

United Services Automobile Association

United Services Automobile Association (USAA) was started in 1922 by military officers who were unable to obtain insurance. The company continues to provide all types of personal insurance, primarily to military officers. While USAA employs approximately 150 retired officers, the large majority of its 5,000 employees are civilians, and 70 percent are female. The association is based in San Antonio, Texas, a city with large military facilities and a climate that favors outdoor leisure activities.

Program Development

In 1971, spurred by increasing public attention to the idea of a shorter workweek, President Robert F. McDermott appointed a study group to determine the feasibility of reducing the workweek through a compressed schedule or other worktime arrangement. McDermott asked the group to come up with a plan that would meet three primary objectives:

- Maintain a high level of service to USAA members;
- Maintain or improve individual productivity levels; and
- Offer substantial benefits to both USAA and the majority of employees.

The group was advised to consider the operational requirements of the company's various departments and the personal needs of employees (e.g., fatigue, transportation, child care, meal time preparation at home). After a period of initial analysis, including an examination of Riva Poor's book *4 Days, 40 Hours,* the study group was expanded to include representatives from all operating areas of the company.

A booklet was printed and distributed to all employees outlining the general policies and practices intended for adoption with the 4-day workweek. The booklet explained how the workday and workweek would be scheduled and the effect of the new arrangement on paid vacation, holidays, sick and personal leave, compensation, and overtime. All employees were then asked, through use of a special questionnaire, to give their personal views of the new schedule, noting preferred hours of work and possible factors of inconvenience (see Exhibit A). Of special concern were the scheduling preferences of working mothers. The questionnaires were returned by 98 percent of the workforce (3,000 employees at that time) and the response was overwhelmingly positive. About 40 employees indicated they might have scheduling problems. (After implementation, 5 of the 40 actually experienced scheduling difficulties and 3 resigned during the first two years because of these problems.) The scheduling preferences noted in the questionnaire were used in forming the worktime guidelines of the USAA program. Just prior to implementation, all employees were asked to read a statement and sign opposite their names if they were willing to work in excess of nine hours per day.

Pilot Program

As the Board of Directors agreed that the 4-day workweek plan appeared to have significant advantages for USAA and employees, it approved implementation of a 90-day trial program. However, due to the wage-price freeze in effect at that time, the start of the trial was delayed. When the U.S. Office of Emergency Preparedness agreed that the program did not, in effect, increase hourly wages by reducing the number of hours in the workweek without reducing salaries, the pilot program went into effect November 15, 1971.

The compressed schedule shortened the workweek from 40 to 38 hours, with no reduction in pay. All categories of employees are included in the plan, with the exception of personnel in computer operations, security and maintenance, and the Mutual Fund and Investment Department. Those in computer operations and security and maintenance, which operate six days per week, 24 hours a day, work three 12.5-hour shifts. The 30 employees in the Mutual Fund and Investment Department, which must by regulation be open and operational on all days the stock market is open, remain on the traditional 40-hour, 5-day workweek.

All other employees work four 9.5-hour days a week (10 hours including one-half hour lunch period). Approximately 70 percent of employees work Monday through Thursday, with the remain-

QUESTIONNAIRE
Four-Day Work Week
USAA

INSTRUCTIONS: Please check the appropriate boxes or complete the blanks on the following questions.

1. Sex
   - ☐ Male
   - ☐ Female

2. Marital Status
   - ☐ Single
   - ☐ Married
   - ☐ Divorced, Widow or Widower

3. Are there children in your household?
   - ☐ Yes—Please indicate their school level(s)
   - ☐ No

   - ☐ Pre-school
   - ☐ Elementary
   - ☐ Junior High/Middle School
   - ☐ Senior High School
   - ☐ College
   - ☐ None of the above

4. Check the location where you work.
   - ☐ Employment Office—Broadway
   - ☐ Main building—Broadway
   - ☐ Rand Building—Downtown
   - ☐ Woodcock Building—Executive Center

5. Under a four-day work week, which of the following hours of work would you prefer? Please indicate your first, second and third choices in the blank spaces opposite each alternative.
   - ____Alternative A: 7:30a.m.—5:30p.m.
   - ____Alternative B: 7:45a.m.—5:45p.m.
   - ____Alternative C: 8:00a.m.—6:00p.m.

6. If your first preference of working hours were adopted, check any of the factors below that would inconvenience your work at USAA.
   ☐ Driving conditions (one car, car pool, etc.)
   ☐ Bus schedule
   ☐ Spouse working
   ☐ Another job
   ☐ Children in school
   ☐ Other (Please Specify)_____
   ☐ None

7. Check any of the alternatives below that would pose an inconvenience great enough to cause you to seek employment elsewhere.
   ☐ Alternative A: 7:30a.m.—5:30p.m.
   ☐ Alternative B: 7:45a.m.—5.45p.m.
   ☐ Alternative C: 8:00a.m.—6:00p.m.
   ☐ None of the work schedules above would pose an inconvenience great enough to cause me to seek employment elsewhere.

Your answers to the questions above will be extremely valuable in helping your association to better serve the future needs of USAA employees. Please return this questionnaire to your supervisor by noon today. Your answers will remain in the strictest of confidence.

United Services Automobile Association USSA Building • 4119 Broadway • San Antonio, Texas 78215 • (512)824-9011

ing 30 percent working a Tuesday through Friday schedule. The workday begins at 7:15 or 7:30 AM and ends at 5:15 or 5:30 PM—the hours chosen by the large majority of employees on the questionnaire.

Adjustments were made to compensate for the decrease in hours worked per week, with the net effect that hours worked per year remain the same as before the 4-day workweek was implemented. Where employees previously received 7.5 paid holidays per year, they now receive none. Employees do observe holidays, but they must work a total of four days each week, even if a holiday falls in the middle of the week. An afternoon coffee break was reduced from 15 minutes to 6 minutes, a morning coffee break was left unchanged. Employees take 30 minutes for lunch. The result of these changes is that employees work the same number of hours per year for the same annual salary, despite the fact that the workweek is reduced (see Exhibit B). Under the compressed workweek arrangement, overtime is handled by paying straight time for the 39th and 40th hours, and time-and-a-half for all hours over 40 for those eligible.

Evaluation

Towards the end of the 90-day trial, an employee opinion questionnaire was distributed to all participating employees. Based on the questionnaire results and other data collected, the Board of Directors determined that the three main objectives had been met and approved McDermott's recommendation that the 4-day workweek become permanent. The decision made USAA the largest company in the United States to have virtually its entire workforce on such a program, according to the Vice President of Personnel Marie B. Kelleher.

An evaluation of the 4-day workweek one year after implementation showed that the program had been even more successful than expected. Employee response remained favorable. The turnover rate was the lowest in 20 years, and only three employees who left their jobs gave the longer workday as a reason. Employees also found that the morning commute was much easier and faster, commuting costs were lower, and child care costs decreased. Employees had 45 more days off per year with no reduction in pay or benefits, and the 3-day weekend was con-

Exhibit B

Comparative Breakdown of Productive Hours

	5-Day Week Ending November 12, 1971		4-Day Week Effective November 15, 1971	
	Wks/days/hrs	Total hours	Wks/days/hrs	Total hours
Gross hours:	52 x 5 x 8	2080	52 x 4 x 9.5	1976
Less paid time off:				
Vacation	11 x 8	88	10 x 9.5	95
Holidays	7.5 x 8	60	- 0 -	0
A.M. coffee break	242 x 15min.	61	198 x 15min.	50
P.M. coffee break	241 x 15min.	60	198 x 6min.	20
Hours worked:		1811		1811

sidered a huge advantage (Exhibit C). There were practically no reports of significantly increased fatigue as a result of the lengthened workday.

USAA also met its objective of maintaining high quality service. During the first year, availability for direct member inquiries increased by 18 percent as a result of the longer workday. Policy turnaround time was reduced by 35 percent, and the total number of complaints from member-policyholders fell. Further, while it had been feared that the longer workday would cause fatigue and lead to an increase in the error ratio in detailed file work, the error ratio actually dropped 15 percent.

Management measured a productivity increase of 1.5 percent; sales increased while the size of the workforce remained the same. Kelleher reports other advantages to the company: decrease in start-up and close-down time, the lowest overtime rate in USAA history, no increase in sick leave, no difference in total annual leave, and the low turnover rate. Additionally, the 4-day week made recruitment easier.

Five years after the plan was started, another evaluation showed that sales were still increasing, turnover was still low (16.4 percent in 1976, compared to 19.9 percent in 1971 and 17.5 percent in 1972), overtime remained at a satisfactory level, productivity held or increased each year, and the 4-day workweek was still a positive recruiting tool.

USAA's shortened workweek, Kelleher observes, has been even more successful than management anticipated. She believes this may be due in part to the careful and extensive study, analysis, and planning that went on for nearly a year before the trial period began. The company has made some changes to facilitate service and further adapt to employees' needs. For example, management has, over time, increased the number of employees on the Tuesday through Friday schedule from 7 percent to 30 percent because of shifts in workload volume. The holiday schedule during the second year was also changed slightly at employees' requests in order to reduce the number of mid-week holidays. Kelleher concludes that overall the program has proved to be of benefit to the company, its employees, and its member-policyholders.

Exhibit C

Employee Opinion Survey
Four-Day Work Week

Part 1.

INSTRUCTIONS: Please check the appropriate box on the following questions.

1. Marital Status
   ☐ Single
   ☐ Married
   ☐ Widow, Widower
      or Divorced

2. Sex
   ☐ Female
   ☐ Male

3. Employment Classification
   ☐ Clerical-Technical-Service
      (Non-Exempt)
   ☐ Administrative Management
      (Exempt)

4. Length of USAA Employment
   ☐ Less than 1 year
   ☐ 1 year to 4 years
   ☐ 5 years to 9 years
   ☐ 10 years or more

5. Age
   ☐ Less than 25
   ☐ 25 to 35
   ☐ 36 to 45
   ☐ 46 or older

6. Primary Work Location
   ☐ Broadway Main Building
   ☐ Rand Building
   ☐ Woodcock Building
   ☐ Employment Center

7. Which of the following groups
   most represents your total annual
   income? (include spouse's
   income if married)
   ☐ Less than $6,000
   ☐ $6,000 to $9,999
   ☐ $10,000 to $14,999
   ☐ $15,000 or more

8. Is your spouse employed?
   ☐ Yes
   ☐ No
   ☐ I am not married

9. Under the four-day work week,
   which is your new day off?
   ☐ Friday
   ☐ Monday
   ☐ Other

10. Which of the following best rep-
    resents the time you begin your
    lunch period?
    ☐ 12:00 Noon to 12:29 P.M.
    ☐ 12:30 P.M. to 12:59 P.M.
    ☐ 1:00 P.M. to 1:30 P.M.
    ☐ Other

11. Please check whichever of the
    following boxes most represents
    your situation regarding children.
    ☐ I have no children
    ☐ I have pre-school children at
       home
    ☐ I have elementary through
       senior high school-age child-
       ren at home
    ☐ I have college-age or older
       children living at home
    ☐ None of my children live at
       home

Part II

INSTRUCTIONS: The following are statements which relate to the Four-Day Work Week at USAA. Please circle the response, opposite the statement, which best describes your feelings about the Four-Day Work Week.

Example:

	Strongly agree 1	Agree 2	Neutral 3	Disagree 4	Strongly disagree 5
No Fault Insurance is a good thing		②			

Compared to a five-day work week, how do you feel about the following aspects of the four-day work week?

	Strongly agree 1	Agree 2	Neutral 3	Disagree 4	Strongly disagree 5
1. I like my job more under the four-day work week	1	2	3	4	5
2. I have not encountered any significant problems created by the four-day work week	1	2	3	4	5
3. I know a great deal about the four-day work week	1	2	3	4	5
4. The longer work day is too exhausting	1	2	3	4	5
5. My spouse/family like the new work schedule more	1	2	3	4	5
6. I am spending more money on my leisure time now	1	2	3	4	5
7. Traffic is heavier to and from work now	1	2	3	4	5
8. I like the time at which I go to lunch	1	2	3	4	5
9. I have more time with my family now	1	2	3	4	5
10. If the decision was made to go back to a five-day work week, I would be upset	1	2	3	4	5
11. I am thinking of moving further away from work now that I have to drive only four days	1	2	3	4	5
12. I get more accomplished at work now	1	2	3	4	5
13. I think the new schedule is a good idea	1	2	3	4	5
14. On the first day of the new work week, I seem more tired than the last work day	1	2	3	4	5
15. If USAA went back to a five-day work week, I would remain a USAA employee	1	2	3	4	5
16. My friends who do not work at USAA think favorably of the four-day work week	1	2	3	4	5
17. I use my new day off for activities I used to take care of during the work week	1	2	3	4	5
18. I am bored with my free time	1	2	3	4	5

Part III

The following two sections (A & B) relate to how you spend your leisure time away from work.

A. WORK DAY - On the normal Work Day, how much time do you spend on each of the following activities during the 14 hours you are not working at USAA? Please circle the number in the column that best describes the time.

EXAMPLE: If you attend one movie during the Four-Day Work Week on your leisure time and the movie lasts 2 hours, then you would circle column 2, less than 1 hr (2 hours per work week for the movie divided by 4 working days equals ½ hour, which belongs in column 2). Make sure that the total number of hours you circle does not exceed 14 hours and that you circle column 1 for each activity on which you spend no time.

	No time	Less than 1 hr	1 hr to 2 hrs	2 hrs to 4 hrs	More than 4 hrs
1. Travel to and from work	1	2	3	4	5
2. Attend sports events (football games, basketball, etc.)	1	2	3	4	5
3. Participate in sports or recreational activities (bowling, golf, swimming, etc.)	1	2	3	4	5
4. Active in the community (church, Boy Scouts, PTA, etc.)	1	2	3	4	5
5. Work at second job	1	2	3	4	5
6. Attend school or do homework	1	2	3	4	5
7. Go to the movies, theater, nightclubs, etc.	1	2	3	4	5
8. Visit relatives or friends	1	2	3	4	5
9. Go shopping	1	2	3	4	5
10. In-the-home activities					
a. Work around the house (repairs, gardening, housework, work on car, etc.)	1	2	3	4	5
b. Watch TV, listen to radio, or read	1	2	3	4	5
c. Hobby activities	1	2	3	4	5
d. Just plain relaxing or loafing	1	2	3	4	5
e. Sleeping	1	2	3	4	5
11. Other than the above	1	2	3	4	5

B. NEW DAY OFF - On the normal **New Day Off** (24 hours Monday or Friday), how much time do you spend on each of the following? Please circle the number in the column that best describes the time. Make sure that the total number of hours you circle does not exceed 24 hours and that you circle column 1 for each activity on which you spend no time.

	No time	Less than 1 hr	1 hr to 2 hrs	2 hrs to 4 hrs	More than 4 hrs
1. Attend sports events (football games, basketball, etc.)	1	2	3	4	5
2. Doctor, dental appointments, etc.	1	2	3	4	5
3. Participate in sports or recreational activities (bowling, golf, swimming, etc.)	1	2	3	4	5
4. Active in the community (church, Boy Scouts, PTA, etc.)	1	2	3	4	5
5. Work at second job	1	2	3	4	5
6. Attend school or do homework	1	2	3	4	5
7. Go to the movies, theater, nightclubs, etc.	1	2	3	4	5
8. Visit relatives or friends	1	2	3	4	5
9. Go shopping	1	2	3	4	5
10. In-the-home activities					
a. Work around the house (repairs, gardening, housework, work on car, etc.)	1	2	3	4	5
b. Watch TV, listen to radio, or read	1	2	3	4	5
c. Hobby activities	1	2	3	4	5
d. Just plain relaxing or loafing	1	2	3	4	5
e. Sleeping	1	2	3	4	5
11. Away-from-the-home activities (traveling, sightseeing, and other than B1 through B10 above)	1	2	3	4	5
12. Other than the above	1	2	3	4	5

Part IV

In the space provided below, please feel free to write any specific comments regarding the Four-Day Work Week which have not been previously covered in this questionnaire. If you have no additional comments, please write the word 'NONE' in the space below.

Thank you for your participation in this important survey. When you have completed the questionnaire, take it personally to the person indicated for your building.

BROADWAY BUILDING:	Give to the receptionist on the first floor by 1:30 P.M.
RAND BUILDING:	Give to Mrs. Bernice Raney on the 7th floor by 12:00 noon
WOODCOCK BUILDING:	Give to Mrs. Patricia Gilmore in Room 2D by 12:00 noon

PART TIME

Bankers Life and Casualty Company

With assets over $1 billion, more than 3,700 home office employees, and nearly 2,000 field workers, Bankers Life and Casualty Company of Chicago ranks in the top 2 percent of insurance companies. Although it has grown rapidly from the small insurance company John D. MacArthur bought in 1935, the company remains committed to community involvement.

Bankers' employees work in more than 30 buildings throughout Chicago, but more are located in the city's Northside, where the company is the largest employer. Because of its proximity to residential neighborhoods, the company has recruited heavily from the community, and many employees regard Bankers as a community enterprise. The company has been actively involved in community projects and has made its resources available for local activities.

Organizational Climate

Bankers is known for its progressive employment policies leading to the more positive utilization of older workers. The President's Committee on the Employment of the Handicapped has recognized the company for its employment of the elderly and handicapped. The City of Chicago has noted its "outstanding contributions on behalf of older and handicapped workers," and a district council of the state's American Legion has cited it for its employment achievements. Bankers also has received extensive media coverage for its policy regarding the continued value of older workers. In addition to coverage by national television networks, Bankers' policies have received international attention; recently, the Japanese Broadcasting Company interviewed and filmed many of the company's older workers as well as discussed Bankers' policies with the company's management.

In its 45-year history, Bankers has never had a mandatory retirement age, and it has had a practice of hiring people in their late 60s and 70s. While most Bankers' employees choose to retire at age 65, approximately 5 percent (170) of its current home office workers are over 65.

When employees do retire, they are made to feel they're "still an important part of the team," says Vice President for Human Resources Dr. Anna Marie Buchmann. The company sends retirees the monthly newsletter and notices about company activities, and they can participate in company social evenings as well as formal programs for long-service employees. Retirees keep their group life insurance, major medical, and basic hospital/medical/surgical/dental coverage if their years of continuous service plus age equal or exceed 75.

Ability to do the job is the sole criterion for employment at Bankers. This philosophy is reflected in the Temporary Workers Pool program established by the company in March 1979. Through this program, the company, when it needs extra help, hires Bankers' retirees directly, helping its operations, avoiding the cost of employment agencies, and providing retirees an opportunity to work at their own convenience on a temporary full-time or part-time basis.

Program Development

The Temporary Workers Pool grew out of another Bankers' project involving retirees. A task force, composed of representatives from Bankers' human resources and training departments, formed in 1978 to develop a preretirement planning seminar for company employees. A research component was conducting a telephone survey of 25 former employees who retired between 1975 and 1978 to ascertain what information and activities would have been useful in planning for their retirement. Some of the retirees expressed regret about their retirement decision; most were enjoying their new lives, but indicated they would like to earn some extra money by working part time.

One of the task force members, Stephen Gilfether, who was then the editor of "Home Office Communications," had become involved in his division's budgetary process and had observed that employment agency fees for temporary workers made up a relatively large budget item. When the results of the telephone interviews were presented to task force members, Gilfether suggested directly hiring Bankers' retirees on a temporary basis. He thought the program would offer several advantages:

- The workers would have known skills and would be familiar with the company's procedures.
- The company would save on employment agency fees.
- Retirees could earn some extra money to supplement their retirement income.
- The plan would demonstrate further Bankers' commitment to hiring older persons.
- Bankers' consideration of retirees as "members of the family" would be demonstrated.
- The plan would respond to community needs.

The task force decided to send a skills inventory and work schedule preference form to all Bankers' annuitants who had retired during the preceding five years to determine their interest in a temporary workers pool. Only 10 retirees who were surveyed responded positively. Company officials attributed this limited interest to two factors: Bankers sent the questionnaire in December, when many retirees were busy with holiday activities and thus not interested in work; and retirees may have been reluctant to register for work during Chicago's bitterly cold winter.

Nevertheless, the idea appealed to top management, and in 1979, an in-house employment agency to register Bankers' retirees for temporary work was established on an experimental basis.

Program Participation

Bankers' retirees interested in the program register with the Human Resources Departments. Previous program coordinator, Minnie Schenker (Schenker decided to retire from Bankers in October of 1980 at age 76) stated that when she received a request for workers, usually a day in advance, she contacted registrants with the appropriate skills. Retirees can choose whether they wish to work; a refusal does not remove their names from the register.

Within a year after its inception, 50 retirees had registered. Of these 10 were the retirees who showed interest initially and the others had signed up for the program before leaving Bankers. According to Schenker, the number of soon-to-retire employees who sign up for the pool has increased because of worries about inflation.

Between March and November 1979, pool workers put in 1,685 hours. Most of the participants are female (reflecting the composition of Bankers' overall workforce which is 73 percent female); four men are involved. Schenker characterized 14 participants as "very active."

Program Administration

Most of the available work is clerical. Wages are varied, depending on the salary level of the particular assignment, but are generally around $4.00 per hour. The company withholds federal and state income tax and social security payments, but retirees do not receive any additional social security benefits or credits. Retirees monitor their earnings closely to ensure that their total annual wages do not exceed the social security earnings ceilings, thus jeopardizing the level of their present benefits.

Evaluation

Initially, managers were skeptical of the program, but they became more favorable once the experiment got underway. To illustrate, a department supervisor estimated he needed six temporary pool workers to work a full day to complete a project; Schenker filled the request within an hour, and the workers completed the job in less than three hours, turning the supervisor into a staunch supporter.

As news of the retirees' efficiency has spread, more departments have been willing to give the temporary workers pool a chance.

Company officials describe the program as a combination of gradual retirement, flexible work schedules, and part-time work. One department even created a "permanent temporary" position. While the company sought a replacement for the full-time receptionist to the executive offices, temporary pool workers filled in. The executive staff were so pleased with the retirees' performance that they decided not to hire a new employee, but to rotate the job among interested pool members. A three-person team now alternates time on the job one week at a time. After each member of the team has worked four weeks, a new team is assigned. This arrangement is structured to allow retirees to plan their work and leisure activities in advance.

Buchmann evaluates the program as very successful, and managers report the quality of work and the retirees' productivity are excellent.

For the retirees, the program provides a way to supplement retirement incomes without their having to commit themselves to full-time work. The program fills their need for activity, provides enjoyment in renewal of social contacts with Bankers' employees, and still allows for leisure time which many participants say they spend with families and grandchildren.

The company obtains the services of experienced, reliable workers without the cost of going through an employment agency. During the first six months, the program saved the company approximately $5,000 in agency fees; after its first full year, the program saved over $10,000 in such fees. The retirees' familiarity with Bankers' way of doing things also eliminates time-consuming and costly orientations.

PART TIME

Boonton Electronics

Located in Parsippany, New Jersey, Boonton Electronics is a small nonunionized manufacturer of electronic test and measurement instruments established in 1947. Boonton's workforce of 183 includes 103 production workers and 80 clerical, professional, and managerial personnel. Males comprise 55 percent of the workforce.

In the past several years, a number of high technology firms have located in the area, creating intense competition among local employers for certain jobs, principally clerks, electronics technicians, and electro-mechanical assemblers. The resulting tight labor market led Boonton to explore various strategies for meeting its labor needs.

Decisionmaking

Company officials explain that successful competition in the field of high-technology equipment depends on production of reliable, high-quality products. Since the company relies heavily on skilled craft workers to achieve consistency in workmanship, retention of skilled workers is a primary objective of Boonton.

Previous experience, gained when several valued employees no longer able to work full time were allowed to work part time, had shown the feasibility of a reduced work hour approach. Now several things suggested that a combined reduced workyear/work hour plan might be successful. Exit interviews with departing employees had revealed interest among many skilled females in continuing to work if the company offered more flexible schedules. The company knew that there were skilled electro-mechanical assemblers in the area interested in working but unwilling or unable to work full time, year-round. Further, many college students were available to work full time during the summers and during Christmas vacations.

Thus, Boonton developed the School Shift Program, designed primarily to recruit mothers and students unable to work full time, year-round, and it was implemented in September of 1978.

School Shift Program

Boonton employs part-time workers from September to June each year. These part-timers are required to work a minimum of five hours each day, but may choose the hours they work. They "quit" each June and are rehired in September if their performance was satisfactory. Employees who find they can continue working during the summer can convert to permanent full-time or permanent part-time status.

Participants in the School Shift Program are considered "temporary" by the company and do not receive the fringe benefits provided to Boonton's permanent employees who work 30 or more hours per week year-round. The company does pay social security, unemployment insurance, and workers' compensation and contributes to the company pension plan if the employee works more than 1,000 hours a year. Program participants also receive holiday pay if they work during a week in which a holiday falls. During the first year in the program, unskilled workers earned $3.60 an hour; skilled workers earned $4.30 an hour. Employees returning in subsequent years receive increases in salary each September.

Participation

Martha Duddy, Personnel Manager, says the program is designed to tap a segment of people unable to work year-round. The advertisement she placed in the local newspaper to recruit potential participants highlighted three points:

- Flexible work hours coinciding with school schedules;
- On-the-job training, no skills required; and
- Ability with finger dexterity needed.

Within a week, Boonton was inundated with applications for the seven positions.

The seven women who participated during the 1978-79 school year worked on wiring, soldering, and mechanical assembly operations. Four returned to the program the following September. Of the others, one became a permanent part-time employee working six hours per day year-round, one became a permanent full-time employee, and the third was not recalled because of poor performance.

In September 1979, there were 10 participants, including 2 male students able to combine work and education. Most of the female participants were mothers of school-age children; however, a few older women with grown children also participated.

Employee Response

Participants who are mothers of elementary school-age children say they did not want to leave their children unsupervised after school. This program provides a feasible means of meeting the dual demands of family and work. They are particularly pleased that the School Shift Program allows them to remain at home when a child is sick or on school vacation without adversely affecting their attendance record.

Although some participants feel exclusion from fringe benefits is unfair (an alternative suggested by some participants is pro-rating benefits according to hours worked), the lack of fringe benefits has not been a major disincentive to participation. For one thing, most participants are covered under their spouses' health and insurance plans. For another, desire for fringe benefits is subordinate to the participants' pride in helping achieve such family goals as buying a house or sending a child to college.

One concern of participants is that the shorter workday makes arranging carpools difficult. Since Boonton is not located near public transportation facilities, some workers who have gone on reduced work hour schedules have had to drive to work alone. As the price of gasoline increases, transportation costs may overshadow the income advantage of working part time.

Overall, participants are enthusiastic about the School Shift Program and have willingly made what many regard as a trade-off between short and long term benefits in order to accommodate current work and family responsibilities.

Effect on Employer

According to company officials, the program has met Boonton's main objectives of:
- Recruiting and retaining skilled workers without a substantial increase in personnel costs;

- Developing and training future full-time workers;
- Achieving greater flexibility in meeting varying production demands;
- Stabilizing the work force;
- Recruiting more mature and dependable skilled employees.

On the basis of the program's success in the production area, the company, in 1979, extended the School Shift Program to the stockroom where turnover was high. The two main reasons for leaving cited by terminating employees were the repetitious nature of the work and the need to stand for a major portion of the day. Boonton restructured the positions so that participants could perform their detailed and repetitious job tasks on a part-time basis. The program resulted in higher job satisfaction and reduced turnover.

Initially, Boonton supervisors were concerned that a reduced workyear approach would cause scheduling and administrative difficulties and would disrupt production. By the end of the first year, the productivity, reliability, and quality of workmanship of the participants convinced them that the program could effectively help them meet production requirements.

Duddy notes that the program has been attractive to women with grown children as well as young mothers because it has let them reenter the work force gradually, building their confidence and employment skills. This confidence is not limited to the employment situation. Many working mothers who start on a part-time, school-year schedule discover that they are able to combine their work and domestic responsibilities. Since its inception in 1978, five School Shift employees have extended their original hours, one has converted to part-time permanent status, and four to full-time permanent status. Boonton's flexitime schedule for full-time workers also benefits part-timers in that part-time work schedules can be arranged throughout a 10.5-hour time span. (The company is open from 7:00 AM until 5:30 PM.)

The problems of underutilized work space and additional paperwork have not been resolved yet. Because of the bench-work method of production, each worker requires a separate work space which cannot be used when the employee is not at work. Paperwork for the Personnel Department has increased since employees are hired part-year. Company officials, however, believe that the benefits of the program have more than offset the associated administrative difficulties.

PART TIME

Control Data Corporation

Based in Bloomington, Minnesota, a suburb of Minneapolis, Control Data Corporation (CDC) is an international corporation with sales exceeding $3 billion. Formed in 1958 as a computer manufacturer, CDC has expanded its operations to include software application services such as programmed educational materials and job matching. It also has diversified through acquisition of firms in such industries as finance, insurance, and automobile leasing.

CDC employs 47,000 people in the United States, 55 percent of whom are male. These cover the full range of occupational categories, from salaried personnel (engineers, programmers, accountants, clerical workers, and other administrative support personnel) to production workers paid by the hour.

Organizational Climate

Over the years CDC has adopted a number of innovative work scheduling arrangements, including flexitime, permanent part time, and paid social service leave. Both a need for workers with specific skills and a management philosophy of moving away from rigid work schedules at the workplace have led to this.

CDC was among the first American companies to introduce flexitime in 1972. The company, in 1979, started a special "Homework" program enabling employees to work at home on a part-time or full-time basis, principally as computer programmers. (The employee communicates via a PLATO computer-based education terminal hooked up to his or her home.) Often these positions have been filled by former CDC employees who had been out of work on a disability. According to Vice President, Corporate Staffing and Personnel Services, Jim Stathopoulos, these employees are pleased with the new work arrangement. Now being implemented is a proposal from CDC's Professional Services Division for a "Work Station Program." Under this program, employees engaged in project-oriented work could work at home or a satellite location, thus reducing employee travel costs and time, increasing productivity, conserving energy, and making more efficient use of company space and equipment.

The company offers paid leave to eligible employees to allow them to become involved in community activities (see chapter 3) and has made special efforts to facilitate the transition from full-time work to retirement by helping retirees arrange consulting relationships with various social and government agencies. CDC also employs older workers and retirees on an in-house consulting basis or in part-time roles. Their special skills and experience are valued in their areas of expertise and in providing career and retirement counseling.

Part-Time Arrangements

CDC has always used part-time employees in most occupational categories. In 1980, the company employed 5,000 part-time workers, with about 20 percent in professional level occupations (e.g., programmers, accountants, and personnel administrators).

Corporate strategy for the 1980s, Stathopoulos says, is to increase the number of part-time personnel. A basic reason for this relatively heavy reliance on part-time personnel is the current and historical shortage of people with skills required by firms in the computer industry. CDC has averaged 800 computer programmer openings at any one time in the past few years.

CDC has arranged part-time schedules around ongoing production requirements as well as peak production demands. Employees may work part-day or part-week, depending on the production needs of the facility. Other schedules are designed around the special needs of employees. One such effort has received widespread coverage in the press and has been cited in books as an innovative approach to job creation for the hard-to-employ. In a low-income neighborhood in St.Paul, Minnesota, CDC constructed a bindery plant staffed primarily by permanent part-time employees (210 part-time and 10 full-time). The bindery's morning shift, from 9:00 AM to 3:00 PM, was designed for mothers of school-age children. The afternoon shift, which starts at 3:00 PM, is for students, and the 4-hour evening shift is staffed principally by students and second wage earners.

The company also employs part-timers who work variable schedules at the job site or at home. For example, employees may be part of a pool of typists of computer programmers who are tapped during production peak loads. The company has the option to use these employees as needed, and the employees may turn down requests to work without prejudice.

Benefits for Permanent Part-Timers

CDC defines permanent part time as regular, voluntary employment carried out during working hours that are shorter than normal but on a year-round basis (i.e., 48 or more weeks). Implementation is flexible; for example, a part-time employee may work 10 hours one week and 40 the next, depending on production needs. CDC does not distinguish between part-time and job sharing positions. The scheduling arrangements of both professional and nonprofessional part-timers are determined by individual needs and department work schedules.

All part-time personnel, including those who work variable hours at home, are eligible for the same benefits as full-time employees with the exception of group health and life insurance. CDC is now negotiating with its insurance companies to provide coverage for part-time employees. Part-timers accrue vacation, holiday, seniority status, and retirement credits on a prorated basis. The Employee Retirement Income Security Act mandates that all employees working for an employer a minimum of 1,000 hours over the course of a year participate in the company-sponsored retirement plan. CDC has lowered the eligibility to 900 hours. Part-timers who work less than 900 hours but at least 500 hours during the year—approximately 10 hours per week—will not have a break in service. This means they will be able to retain previous years of service credited to their retirement plan. However, they will not receive as credit a year of service for that particular year.

Part-time personnel, under a current proposed policy change, will be eligible for all employee services, including personal loans, training programs, and employee stock purchase plans.

Promotion Policy

It is CDC's policy that all employees receive the same pay for the same work, observes Stathopoulos, who also notes wage increases and performance appraisal procedures for full-time employees are applied to part-timers. Performance standards that have been designed for job classifications in CDC apply to part-time employees as well as full-timers in the same job family. The performance of all employees is reviewed annually.

Cost/Benefits Associated with Part-Time Employment

CDC managers report that their experience is at variance with generally accepted beliefs about permanent part-time arrangements—high costs for fringe benefits, recruiting and training, scheduling difficulties, work flow problems, and administrative complications. At CDC, management believes that available technology minimizes certain costs and that the benefits of drawing from a permanent pool of part-timers outweigh other costs. For example, all CDC administrative systems (e.g., budget, personnel) are computerized. Personnel and work scheduling are easily managed through the company's automated systems. Managers also consider it relatively easy for supervisors to direct part-time subordinates at the lowest level of supervision where small numbers of employees are supervised.

Although they have not studied the matter in detail, managers consider part-time employees to be highly productive because they are job directed and focused when at work.

Stathopoulos adds that by relying on part-time personnel, CDC's facilities are able to tap the local labor market (principally of homemakers, older persons, and students), thereby minimizing nationwide advertising and relocation costs.

In the past, CDC hired part-time help through temporary employment agencies. A number of problems arose: one manager, for example, reported that in using temporary help, 50 percent of the referrals had to be sent home because of inappropriate or inadequate skills. Another factor that impeded the productivity of temporary employees was the lack of knowledge about CDC's systems, procedures, and terminology. Management has concluded that, even with the added fringe benefit costs, maintaining a pool of permanent part-time employees is less costly overall.

PART TIME

United California Bank

United California Bank, a nonunionized financial institution, is the fifth largest bank in southern California with more than 316 branches and 13,000 employees. Close to 75 percent of its workforce is female, primarily young women in entry-level clerical positions and older married women supplementing family income.

Part-Time Arrangements

To meet the different staffing demands necessitated by workflow variations, United California Bank employs large numbers of part-time workers.

In 1974, the company began to explore approaches that might reduce its high turnover rate. One step in the process was a workforce analysis, which revealed that many part-time employees worked nearly 30 hours a week. Management met with these workers and learned that the unavailability of fringe benefits was a factor contributing to turnover.

The following year, to reduce turnover and increase retention of qualified employees, United California Bank restructured its part-time employment into two categories:

- Part-time hourly workers. Employees work fewer than 20 hours a week and receive hourly wages. They are eligible to participate in the company's medical-dental insurance plan (their dependents are not eligible) and receive vacation leave prorated according to the number of hours worked. United California Bank employed approximately 500 part-time hourly employees in 1978.

- Modified full-time employees. Employees working more than 20 hours per week are eligible for the same benefits as full-time employees: life insurance, medical-dental insurance for themselves and their dependents, pension benefits, and, for those working more than 24 hours a week, long-term disability insurance. Vacation and sick leave are prorated according to the number of hours worked each week. In 1978, the bank employed approximately 900 workers on this schedule.

Effect on Employer

In providing fringe benefits to its part-time employees, United California Bank encountered two major problems. First, the bank's insurance coverage is provided through a holding company which also provides benefits to a number of other organizations. Before the plan could be modified to include part-time workers, the consent of other affected companies was needed. The negotiations took considerable time.

Second, United California Bank's records on fringe benefits for its employees were maintained on 13-year-old computer software not designed to provide prorated benefits for part-time workers. Changing the original software was a complicated procedure and caused time-consuming administrative difficulties for management and part-time employees.

Despite these problems, the program has had some positive results. While the bank has not performed any rigorous evaluation of the two part-time categories, the options have, according to Vice President and Manager of Compensation and Benefits, Donald H. Smith, helped reduce hiring and training costs and retain some skilled personnel.

Although turnover remains higher than the company would like, the rate is significantly lower for modified full-time workers than for hourly part-timers. Overall, management believes the switch to the two arrangements has assisted in meeting the bank's variable workflow in a cost-efficient manner.

PART TIME

Maryland State Automobile Insurance Fund

The Maryland State Automobile Insurance Fund is a state agency created in 1973 by an act of the Maryland state legislature as a result of a law mandating automobile insurance for all automobiles registered in the state. Headquartered in Annapolis, with three field offices, the Fund's main purpose is to issue automobile insurance policies to motorists unable to obtain insurance through private carriers. Any resident motorist who is turned down by two major automobile insurance companies is eligible for insurance through the state agency, providing they have a valid Maryland driver's license.

The Fund has approximately 500 employees. About half of the work in the Claims Department is investigating and processing accident claims. Approximately 100 employees in the Underwriting Department issue policies, and the remainder are in Administrative Support Departments (e.g., Fiscal, Personnel, Computer), most in clerical positions.

Fewer than 25 percent of Fund employees are represented by unions. These are represented either by the American Federation of State, County and Municipal Employees (AFSCME) or by the Maryland Classified Employees Association (MCEA), a union that represents government in Maryland.

Program Origin

In 1975, the Maryland state legislature passed a law mandating the establishment of permanent part-time positions in departments in the Executive Branch. The original legislative intent was: to retain skilled workers; to attract skilled workers from among people who couldn't work full time; and to improve productivity in state government.

Fund management set up the program in 1978 within the broad guidelines provided by the Maryland State Personnel Office. Initially, information about the program was communicated to employees through the employee newspaper; included was a survey asking employees to indicate whether they were interested in converting from a full-time to a part-time schedule.

As positions become vacant, the Fund's personnel office suggests to supervisors that they consider hiring a part-time person or job sharing team to fill the slot.

The Personnel Office has authority for determining which positions can be filled by part time or job sharing. Theoretically, the program is open to all employees. In actuality, there are some positions deemed inappropriate by the Personnel Office. Officials have evaluated the position of private secretary, for example, as one requiring continuity and therefore have recommended against it being filled on a part-time or job sharing basis. Further, they believe supervisory jobs must be full time. On the other hand, they do encourage part-time workers in typing pool positions, as they believe they can be more productive than full-timers.

Participation

In 1980, 10 people participated in the part-time program. (Job sharing is permitted under the 1975 law but, so far, no employees are working under this arrangement.) This number has been relatively constant since the program's inception in 1978.

Most of the permanent part-time positions are clerical. As the agency needs more people in the mornings to open mail, a number of the part-timers work mornings in mail room facilities. Many part-timers are women, aged 25 to 35 years, with young children. The agency permitted one mother to work part time during the summer when her children were out of school and then to return full time in the fall.

Fringe Benefits/Promotions

State fringe benefit and promotion policies apply to the Fund. Part-time employees are eligible for fringe benefits on a prorated basis. To be eligible for prorated retirement benefits, they must work between 50 and 80 percent of full-time hours. The state computes retirement benefits on the average salary of the three highest year earnings. Employees are promoted according to their full-time equivalency years of employment; for example, a person working 50 percent must work twice the number of years required of a full-timer to be eligible for promotion.

Recruitment

The part-time program is communicated statewide through the Maryland State Personnel Office. The Fund gets the names of potential part-time workers from the state and hires applicants from the state eligible list.

The Fund's Personnel Manager, Thomas H. Dixon III, says that recruiting part-timers presents more problems than recruiting for full-time positions. He notes that frequently the Fund determines the hours and days suitable for a specific part-time position and then sets out to fill the position. However, those people desiring part-time employment can't always work the particular schedule. The Fund then may interview 10 eligible candidates for every part-time position as opposed to 5 for a full-time slot.

Dixon also states that job applicants may view part-time employment as a way "to get a foot in the door" for state employment. Once situated, many switch to full-time employment.

Administration

Within the Fund, the program is administered by the Personnel Office, with the Personnel Manager overseeing the program. There is no coordinator of part-time employees.

The Maryland State Personnel Office, by virtue of the 1975 law, has responsibility for implementing and evaluating the program. State law requires that the State Personnel Office collect an annual report from each agency documenting the number of part-time positions and, among other requirements, explaining a failure to fill a certain number of positions. The law further empowers the State Personnel Office to work with individual agencies to assist with recruitment and carry out the program.

Reactions To The Program

Program participants have responded very favorably. Supervisory resistance had been strong initially, as there was fear that filling a full-time position with a part-timer would mean the permanent loss of the rest of the position, thus, hindering the efforts of a unit to complete its work function. It soon became apparent that part-timers were able to complete an amount of work comparable to their percentage of time worked. If necessary, supervisors were able to hire additional part-time employees. There has been little feedback from the unions, according to Dixon.

Dixon believes the program probably will continue on the same basis as the past two years. He does not foresee a large-scale expansion effort, but says that the size will continue to be based upon the needs of the agency.

JOB SHARING

State of Wisconsin

The development of job sharing in Wisconsin's civil service can be traced to two separate but related events that occurred during 1976. The first was the establishment by the Wisconsin State Legislature of a task force to analyze job sharing and flexible work hours. The task force recommendations led to passage of legislation in 1978 mandating state agencies to experiment with flexible work hours and to increase the number of permanent part-time—including job sharing—opportunities available to Wisconsin's 36,000 employees. Currently, 25 percent of Wisconsin's state employees are covered by a flexitime plan, and 7.8 percent are working on a permanent part-time basis.

The second was a two-and-a-half year research and demonstration study, funded by the U.S. Department of Labor, to examine and test the feasibility of job sharing at the professional and paraprofessional level in the Wisconsin state civil service system.

Project JOIN Implementation

The DOL funds to develop and test job sharing resulted in the creation of Project JOIN (Job Options and Innovations). JOIN's objectives were to develop job sharing positions in Wisconsin's state government and to research them in terms of productivity, job satisfaction, cost, and characteristics of job sharers. JOIN also was to determine whether this scheduling option had particular value for women, handicapped, and older workers.

There were two components of the project: research, through the University of Wisconsin's Department of Economics; and implementation, through the State Department of Employment Relations.

According to Project JOIN, job sharing is the employment of two people in a position that was formerly full time through a reorganization of tasks. JOIN provides definitions of two ways to job share:

Job Pairing: Two people share one full-time job with equal responsibilities for the total job. Each works half time; together they provide full-time coverage.

Split Level: Two people share one full-time job. Each works half time. Duties are divided into a different skill and pay level for each person.

Under the co-direction of Mary Cirilli and Diane Jones, Project JOIN attempted to systematically survey state employees to determine interest in reduced work schedule positions, identify obstacles to shared job employment, assess costs, involve groups representing affected employees, identify positions that would lend themselves to job sharing, conduct task analysis, work out equitable fringe benefit packages, and conduct educational and recruitment activities.

- Survey. Of 28,000 full-time state employees surveyed, 6 percent expressed a desire to work part time at some point in their career, with 3 percent stating an immediate need for such employment.

- Job Identification and Analysis. Project staff, working with state personnel officers, first identified positions that might be amenable to job sharing. Project staff then divided the position into its various components so that two part-time or shared positions would result. "This task analysis," says Project Assistant Kathryn Moore, "was an absolutely crucial step in defining the new job sharing positions." Additionally, staff worked with survey respondents who had indicated a desire to reduce their work hours and whose supervisors agreed the reductions were feasible.

- Fringe Benefits. In conjunction with the Division of Personnel and the State Department of Employee Trust Funds, JOIN staff determined that Wisconsin law does not mandate an across-the-board prorating of fringe benefits for part-time work. Persons interested in job sharing were fully informed as to what benefits were available: for persons working 1,044 hours or more a year, these included full health insurance and prorated vacation, sick leave, holidays, and retirement benefits. For example, a full-time employee with five years' service is entitled to 15 vacation days a year; an employee working a half-time schedule is entitled to 7.5 days. Job sharers are required to work at least 16 hours in weeks in which national holidays fall. If a job sharer's workday falls on a holiday, the sharer is expected to work another day that week. All state employees, full time and part time, must fill out leave slips for vacation and personal holidays.

- Advisory Board. A 16-member board, representing state agencies, public employee unions, community-based organizations, and state legislators, was established as an ongoing vehicle for information and general acceptance.

- Information Campaign. Staff presented information on job sharing to the State Personnel Management Association. JOIN staff also prepared and distributed a brochure describing the program's intent to all state agencies. Further, Wisconsin's Secretary of the Department of Administration sent a statement of support to the heads of all state agencies.

- Recruitment. When the Department of Personnel announced the job sharing vacancies, special note was made that the positions were shared jobs and sharers would be required to answer questionnaires as part of a research effort. JOIN staff identified recruitment networks and contacted, individually and through organizations, the three primary target groups—women, older workers, and the handicapped.

Participation

JOIN exceeded its goal of developing 50 shared (25 full-time) professional and paraprofessional positions within Wisconsin's civil service by creating 59 full-time positions (118 shared jobs). Classifications included attorneys, registered nurses, microbiologists, electronics technicians, curators, training officers, social workers, analysts, and library assistants.

Of the final 118 job sharers, 73 were former full-time civil service workers. More than 370 people (some from outside the government) sought reduced work schedule employment; 49 percent of these now work full time. Diane Jones observes that some people are working full time because it is the only scheduling option available. "It is clear that allowing persons now working full time to reduce their work hours would have significant impact on the unemployment rate," she concludes.

The characteristics of the job sharing participants, as well as of the applicants whose resumes remain on file, show women as most interested in permanent part-time and shared positions. Females with children under six show the greatest preference. JOIN also found the existence of other family income played a determining role in individual preference for part-time employment.

Participation in Project JOIN is 76 percent female and 24 percent male. Sharers have an average of 16 years education and an average of 11 years work experience.

Among those employed in shared positions are five handicapped persons who were unable to work full time because of a disability. Some of these persons were already working for the state and reduced their work hours; others were recruited from the outside. Mary Cirilli says that organizations for handicapped persons showed "high interest" in job sharing during the development phase.

Older workers evidenced interest in job sharing when initially surveyed, yet their actual participation was low. Approximately 50 percent of those state workers aged 55 or older who responded to the survey indicated an interest in alternative work patterns but were hesitant to participate because they did not know what the impact would be on their retirement benefits. (See chapter 3 for a description of Wisconsin's Pre-Retirement Options Project, a program offshoot for older workers.)

Of the total number of JOIN participants, 25 terminated from the program for personal or financial reasons. A few cited scheduling difficulties. In the latter case, supervisors and workload demands dictated a job sharing schedule which was not advantageous to the job sharer.

Evaluation

Citing lower turnover and sick leave usage and increased job satisfaction and productivity for many of the job sharers, Cirilli and Jones emphasize that the project points to the overall benefits of job sharing. Project results are detailed in JOIN's final report to the U.S. Department of Labor. Following are some key findings:

- Turnover and sick leave usage were lower for job sharers than for their full-time counterparts.

- Job satisfaction appeared to be highest among job sharers. However, two different measurements were used to compare satisfaction, one of which showed higher satisfaction for sharers while the other showed no significant difference.

- Training took more supervisory time for sharers, but JOIN found this was an initial cost that ended once the employees were trained. In situations where full-time employees reduced their schedules, little or no training was needed.

- The cost of employing two job sharers was $1,472 less than the cost of employing one full-time worker. Costs included in the analysis were health insurance, life insurance, social security, retirement benefits, and salaries. On the average, salaries were lower for job sharers, either because the jobs were split into differential skill levels or some job sharers were new employees who started at the bottom of the pay range. Benefit costs were slightly higher since Wisconsin offers the same contribution to health insurance for full-and part-time employees. Approximately 55 percent of the job sharers elected to take health insurance. After figuring in costs associated with sick leave usage, turnover, and training, JOIN staff concluded the costs of employing job sharers is about the same as employing full-timers.

- Higher productivity was attributed to former full-time state employees who reduced their hours. The evaluation found no discernible difference in the productivity of job sharers hired from outside civil service and comparable full-time employees.

Special Considerations

Project JOIN staff state that planning is a key step in successful implementation of a job sharing arrangement. They note, though, that even with their extensive planning, certain unanticipated problems as well as advantages arose during implementation.

• Supervisory Support. According to Co-Director Jones, "the positive support of the supervisor can often determine the success of a shared position. The supervisor's role is critical in dividing work, scheduling, communication, resolving difficulties, and evaluating the job sharing team." JOIN staff advised supervisors of benefits and problems associated with job sharing at the start of the program but feel that training was insufficient. When JOIN staff asked 36 supervisors of job sharers whether they would refill the position with two part-time or one full-time employee if both sharers left, 17 said they would revert to one full-time employee, 14 said they would continue with job sharers, and 5 indicated no preference. Supervisors who would revert to full-time employees voiced concerns that job sharing took too much interviewing and training time, required additional work space, and lacked continuity that was required in particular positions. Some observed that half-time people weren't as involved in their jobs as full-time workers and positions involving heavy travel weren't suited to job sharing. On the other hand, a supervisor satisfied with the job sharing arrangements noted: "One positive and quite unexpected spin-off which we have noticed is that our office has been forced to reexamine and streamline certain processes and abandon or transfer others. It's possible that this wouldn't have occurred if the job sharers hadn't observed how much time they were spending on routine paper-shuffling. Apparently, one gets a better view of what constitutes 'wasted' effort for a 4-hour per day perspective."

• Scheduling. Work schedules varied widely to meet the particular situation of each position. The most common schedules were two days of work followed by three days off one week, and then three days of work with two days off the next week; half days every day; and two-and-one-half days at work each week. Other schedules included one full week at the job followed by a full week at home; one, three, or six months at work with one, three, or six months off; or some variation.

Once the project was underway, JOIN staff observed that certain schedules were more appropriate for some jobs than others. For example, half-day schedules were found inappropriate for jobs requiring extensive travel; a schedule requiring five full days a week was more efficient. The most successful schedules for sharers in public contact jobs were half days every day; full days alternating days; or 5-hour days four days a week. Staff also found that a six month on/off schedule was appropriate for parole officers and counselors, or others in high-pressure jobs, who experience burnout. An evaluation conducted by the supervisor of a shared Probation Officer position, for example, showed the shared arrangement did not negatively affect the clients being served.

• Communication. Job sharers and their supervisors relied on a variety of techniques, including charts and records, notes, phone, staff meetings, and overlap time. Sharers and supervisors agreed that the success of the methods depended largely on good planning.

• Unions. Wisconsin's state employees are represented by the American Federation of State, County and Municipal Employees and the American Federation of Teachers. Labor's attitude about part-time employment was mixed, even within the same union. A representative from each of the unions served on the JOIN Advisory Board. The representative from AFT's Local 3271 said that some AFT officials view expanded part-time opportunities as a step toward achieving fuller employment goals and a larger union membership; they believe that part-timers would show a greater attachment to the union once AFT responded to the needs of members desiring reduced work schedules. Other officials within the local believe that part-time workers would be less committed both to their jobs and the union. Both unions decided to charge part-time members approximately half the membership dues required for full-time workers.

• Promotion/Career Advancement. According to Co-Director Cirilli, job sharers have limited access to career advancement opportunities. One reason is the limited number of high level permanent part-time positions. Another is that most higher-level positions involve supervisory responsibility, and this is an area in which few job sharing arrangements have been tried. Administrators are reluctant to allow sharing in supervisory positions because they assume it cannot work and there are few models to cite. The most difficult barrier to overcome, Cirilli observes, is the negative stereotype associated with part-time employment, i.e., a part-time employee is not serious or committed to his/her job and therefore not a good candidate for a higher-level position.

Each permanent part-time employee is eligible to be considered for a merit increase. Wisconsin state part-time employees have an opportunity for advancement to higher-level positions through reclassifications, provided their duties have expanded to warrant a higher level.

Conclusion

Project JOIN found job sharing a feasible arrangement in a number of employment situations. Although staff found that some jobs—particularly those involving substantial travel—were not amenable to sharing, they were able to resolve problems in continuity, for example, by setting a different job sharing schedule. Cirilli and Jones stress that job sharing is one of a number of personnel methods for recruiting competent employees, increasing worker satisfaction, and reducing turnover and absenteeism, and observe that it is appropriate in many more situations than previously imagined.

PART TIME, JOB SHARING

Madison Public Library

The City of Madison, Wisconsin's Public Library is open 72 hours each week. The library, a quasi-independent agency serving a population of 170,000, is organized into six divisions operating out of the main library plus 11 field units. The library director, its chief executive officer, reports to a board of nine members who are appointed by the Mayor and confirmed by the City Council. Library positions are covered by the city's civil service system; hence, the library director and supervisors must follow all civil service rules and regulations regarding personnel actions. Although most city agencies are represented by unions, library employees, with the exception of custodians and full-time bookmobile drivers, are not unionized.

Part-Time Status

Budgeted for 138 full-time equivalent positions, the library is staffed by 250 employees—a ratio of nearly 2 employees for each full-time position. Approximately 85 percent of the library's workforce is female.

In addition to full-time permanent employees and some limited-term personnel, the library employs the following types of part-time workers:

- Hourly employees. These employees do not have civil service status. The generally work 10 to 15 hours a week as pages, emergency drivers, and so forth, mostly at minimum wages and with no benefits except social security. Most are high school and college students.
- Permanent Part Time. These employees have civil service status and receive all benefits of a full-time employee on a prorated basis. In 1979, the library employed 23 permanent part-timers. (More details about fringe benefits follow.)
- Job Sharers. Also civil servants receiving a prorated share of fringe benefits, the job sharers filled eight positions in 1979.

Impetus for Job Sharing

Permanent part-time positions have been part of the library personnel system for more than two decades. These positions were created to meet the needs of the branch libraries, which are open long and irregular hours, and to stretch the library's budget.

In 1973 a number of factors converged to promote adoption of job sharing arrangements. A resolution was introduced in the City Council to require city agencies to set aside a specified number of positions for job sharing, for the dual purpose of creating jobs and accommodating people's needs and lifestyles. Madison's Affirmative Action Officer was promoting more city jobs for women. Additionally, the library's professional workforce had signed a petition requesting the creation of job sharing positions.

Although Madison's Mayor supported the principle of job sharing, he opposed the City Council resolution because he felt the requirement of a specified number of positions was too rigid for agency managers. He proposed instead to create job sharing positions through administrative action. Library Director Bernard Schwab, who had seen the petition requesting job sharing, offered to use the library as a test case. The first two job sharing positions were created at the library in 1974.

Distinctions between Permanent
Part Time and Job Sharing

The difference between permanent part time and job sharing at the library is the ease with which positions can be switched between full time and part time.

Burdensome administrative procedures are required to convert jobs classified as part time to full-time positions. Job sharing positions, on the other hand, are classified as full time and can be changed back and forth easily at the discretion of the director. Various options exist for management and employees on the use of job sharing positions. For example, if a vacancy occurs in a shared position, the director can evaluate whether it should be filled with another part-timer or converted into one full-time position. When a part-time vacancy occurs, the employee filling the other part of the shared job may elect to continue on the job full time, provided the employee previously worked full time.

There are two types of job sharing positions—job splitting and job pairing. In job splitting, the full-time position is broken into discrete tasks; one employee performs one set of tasks and the other performs the others. Essentially, they are permanent part-time positions with the flexibility of being converted to full-time without complications. Job pairing positions are those involving interdependence and requiring continuity. The same tasks are performed by both employees, but one is designated the senior partner.

Consideration

Problems or difficulties associated with scheduling, communication, compatibility, and accountability are more likely to occur in job pairing since it requires a close working relationship and much coordination between the two partners, says Schwab.

- Scheduling. Work schedules vary. They must meet the dual criteria of meeting the needs of the public and the employees. Among schedules that have been used at the library are: half days; full days, with two days on and three days off one week, then three days on and two days off the next; and split weeks, with two-and-one-half days on and two-and-one-half days off.

- Communication. Once the schedule is determined, management and employees work out appropriate means of communication (written, oral, staff meetings, and home phone calls). Effective communication between job pairers has been less of a problem than communication between job pairers and their supervisors and co-workers. One supervisor mentions several problems that have occurred in her office: she feels she has an additional burden because she needs to issue directions and instructions to both members of the team; sometimes an activity is delayed until the second sharer is told; at times, an employee from another unit seeking an answer or decision has had to wait two or three days until the senior partner returns to work.

Schwab notes that the solution to communication problems usually is not sought through rescheduling because of the likelihood that the change would conflict with service or employees' needs. Management is more likely to rework the job duties so that communication requirements are kept to a minimum.

- Accountability. The library mandates that some paired positions, particularly those involving professionals and supervisors, be constructed so that one of the employees has a higher rank and is identified as the senior partner. This senior partner is accountable for the work of the team (and for any others working for the pair) and also is responsible for training the junior partner. Interviews with Schwab, a library supervisor, and two job pairing teams indicate that junior partners do not resent this arrangement. They explain that from the start, a clear distinction is made and the duties of each partner are delineated. Senior partners previously have held full-time positions at the library and have initiated the job pairing arrangement. Although they need not be, junior partners thus far have been new hires and, as such, have been willing to accept their subordinate roles.

- Fringe Benefits. Part-time employees and job sharers with civil service status are eligible to receive all benefits of full-time employees, though generally on a prorated basis. They pay a higher percentage of the premiums relative to the city's share of health insurance costs than their full-time counterparts. Schwab notes that of 40 part-timers (permanent and limited term) and job sharers, 16 carry insurance, 24 do not. Many are married women who prefer to be covered under their husbands' plans.

Evaluation

Schwab says job sharing has had several benefits. It has enabled the library to retain valuable employees. Morale among employees has improved as reduced work hour schedules have accommodated employees' personal and family needs. Schwab also points to the larger societal benefit through the creation of jobs.

He grants, however, that the library has reached a saturation point in terms of part-time personnel, with the nearly two employees for each full-time position. Administration has grown more complex and Schwab feels accountability and communication would suffer with an increase in part-time employees.

PART TIME, JOB SHARING

Hewlett-Packard

Hewlett-Packard (HP) is a major designer and manufacturer of precision electronic equipment for measurement, analysis, and computation. The company was founded in 1939 in Palo Alto, California by two Stanford engineering school graduates and friends, William Hewlett and David Packard. During its first 20 years, the company concentrated on developing electronic testing and measuring equipment for engineers and scientists. Since then, HP has expanded its product line to include computers, calculators, medical electronic equipment, solid state components, and instrumentation for chemical analysis. Altogether, it markets about 4,000 products.

An international company, HP has plants in 18 cities in the United States and 8 cities overseas. In 1980, it added about 10,000 employees, bringing its workforce to more than 57,000. Minorities represented 18 percent and women 42 percent of HP's total U.S. employment. Annual sales reached $3.1 billion.

Organizational Climate

The basic philosophy by which the company operates has been termed "the HP way." The policies, actions, and traditions that characterize the HP way evolved over the years under Hewlett and Packard's leadership. Among the concepts embodying the HP way are:

- Respect for the individual
- Recognition of individual achievement
- Management trust in and understanding of employees
- Management by objective
- Individual employee freedom in attaining well-defined company objectives
- Opportunity for employees to assume greater responsibilities

HP's operations are decentralized. The company's basic units, its product divisions, are kept relatively small and well-defined in order to give employees a clear sense of their mission and their individual contributions to overall performance. Underlying HP's personnel policies is the concept of sharing—sharing responsibilities for defining and meeting goals, sharing the profits, and sharing the opportunity for personal and professional growth.

Innovative Approaches

In this climate, the company was one of the first in the country to institute flexitime. Having developed a successful program in its plant in Germany, HP began a flexitime experiment in 1972 in its Waltham, Massachusetts facility. The program was very successful and HP expanded it throughout the company. By 1980, more than 80 percent of all employees—both manufacturing and managerial workers—at 22 separate facilities worldwide were participating.

In 1970, the company was faced with a 10 percent layoff when the company's orders declined during a general industry slowdown. Consistent with its commitment to job security and philosophy of sharing, HP instituted a work sharing plan for all its employees. Between December 1970 and June 1971, approximately 10,000 salaried and production workers in 15 American facilities went on a reduced schedule of working 9 days out of 10 in a 2-week period. Employees received every other Friday off and a concomitant 10 percent reduction in pay.

The company was pleased to have avoided layoff and loss of valued employees, and to have had in place a highly qualified workforce when business improved.

Also reflecting HP corporate values are the permanent part-time and job sharing arrangements within the company. Although the extent of such arrangements is not closely monitored, Personnel Manager Frank Williams estimates there were 300 permanent part-time and 25 job sharing arrangements within the company in 1980. Headquarters designs personnel policies to provide local supervisors with the flexibility to develop arrangements that meet their office needs.

Three desires motivate HP managers to implement such arrangements:

- Retain highly qualified employees who can no longer work full-time schedules;

- Recruit employees with specific needed skills;
- Meet affirmative action goals.

According to Williams, there is one disincentive to the expansion of such arrangements at HP: for accounting purposes, HP's personnel ceiling is based on head count rather than on a full-time equivalency basis. This sometimes can discourage supervisors since they are budgeted for only a certain number of positions.

Part-time workers employed more than 20 hours per week are eligible to participate fully in HP's benefit package. Vacation, sick leave, and disability pay for part-time workers are prorated according to the numbers of hours worked.

Williams says that job sharing at HP seems to work effectively in more routine positions for which job tasks are clearly defined and can be split between two people. HP's experience with job sharing at professional levels indicates that positions having a high degree of responsibility are difficult to share. HP has had more success when this type of job is restructured into a permanent part-time position.

Although permanent part time and job sharing are not extensive at HP, Williams senses that supervisors are becoming more receptive to these modified work hour arrangements and believes further implementation can be expected.

JOB SHARING

TRW Vidar

TRW Vidar is a nonunionized telecommunications firm in Sunnyvale, California, founded in 1957. In 1975, TRW Inc. acquired Vidar as an operating division within their expanding electronics group. Vidar now employs 1,460 people, of whom 50 percent are female.

Its situation is similar to other advanced technology firms in California's "Silicon Valley" in that it faces stiff competition in recruiting and retaining employees. Recruitment pressure has stimulated interest by these firms in a variety of innovative personnel policies.

Background

In November 1977, Vidar began experimenting with job sharing. Two full-time employees were permitted to share the responsibilities and salary of Personnel Representative. Cris Piasecki and Nancy Creamer together combined eight years of full-time work experience with the company when they requested a change to job sharing. Piasecki, with a degree in personnel administration, was Personnel Representative to Vidar's Compensation and Staffing Supervisor. Committed to a career in personnel, Creamer had moved from a secretarial job to Personnel Assistant reporting to the Industrial Relations Manager.

Both women were interested in combining career and parenting. They had discussed job sharing casually as a way to balance these dual demands, but only when they became pregnant at about the same time did they begin to explore seriously the feasibility of sharing a job at Vidar. They researched the issue and wrote a proposal in which they analyzed specific job tasks for Personnel Representative, outlined employer advantages, and addressed such management concerns as communications, supervision, benefits, and pay.

The reaction of their supervisors was mixed. On one hand, the supervisors were interested in an approach that would allow the company to retain two valued, productive, and experienced employees. On the other hand, both supervisors had serious reservations about the effects of job sharing on the department's functions, particularly about loss of control, poor communications resulting in inadequate service to Vidar managers, and work "falling through the cracks."

After some weeks of consideration, the supervisors proposed a compromise: two separate part-time positions, with Creamer in Employee Relations and Piasecki in Employment. However, while Creamer was on maternity leave, recruitment demands in the Personnel Department increased considerably. This led to a reevaluation and, ultimately, a decision to convert the full-time position of Personnel Representative to a shared job.

Arrangement

The duties of the shared Personnel Representative position include recruiting, screening, interviewing, and hiring job applicants. Initially, the sharers divided the job functions, with Creamer recruiting nonexempt clerical workers and Piasecki recruiting nonexempt technical and exempt administrative personnel. But this division wasn't realistic, according to Piasecki, as the two ended up working on whatever tasks were most pressing, thereby overlapping functions. In December 1978, Vidar's management acknowledged the two as one team handling the same employment openings—a more natural approach.

When the job sharing arrangement began, each sharer worked four hours a day, with a half-hour overlap at the middle of the day. In 1980, they changed the schedule to work a split workweek, with a half-hour overlap on Wednesdays.

While their hours are evenly divided, salaries are not. Creamer, the less experienced team member, receives a lower salary. Available benefits are prorated accordingly.

Ways of Handling Potential Problems

Communications. Three out of the four Vidar managers Piasecki interviewed in 1980 to assess management response to the job sharing arrangement felt that communication is the greatest potential problem in job sharing, though they believed many of the problems were solvable. They commented that priorities are not always discussed in detail and that one of the team may be better informed than the other.

In the beginning, the job sharers had to insist firmly that Vidar managers speak to whomever was on duty about all issues. Some managers were confused by the team concept; others wanted to talk to the person they had contacted first. Piasecki and Creamer explained the job sharing arrangement to managers and co-workers and stressed their interchangeability. Once people became accustomed to the arrangement, communication became easier. To facilitate the team approach, they share one desk and have one business card bearing both names.

The sharers communicate by overlapping worktime and through memos, meetings, and telephone calls to clarify ideas and wrap up loose ends. Their supervisor, Bill Connolly, Recruitment and Staffing Manager, recognizes the need for good communication and spends time meeting with each sharer individually as well as together.

Performance Evaluation and Promotion. Often, one of the team starts a project and the other completes it. The team's first supervisor had little trouble appraising their performance since he had worked with both when they were full-time employees. Connolly, later appointed supervisor, reports he had some difficulty determining which one of the team did what job but has overcome the problem by assigning each sharer individual projects, while they continue to work as a team on day-to-day recruiting assignments.

Connolly has not identified other positions in the department to which Piasecki and Creamer can move as a team. Special consideration must be given to each individual's skill level and career goals.

Administration. Finding an efficient and reliable means of evaluating performance and communicating with two sharers does take extra supervisory effort, according to Connolly.

Fringe Benefits. Connolly says that working out a prorated benefits program has been difficult. In 1977, Vidar's benefit program excluded part-time employees, so neither sharer received any fringe benefits at first. In February 1978, Vidar changed its personnel policy to include prorated sick leave, holiday, and vacation for all part-time employees working more than 20 hours a week. Connolly asked Piasecki to compile a cost justification for dental, health, and life insurance that would equal the cost of the same benefits for one employee. And, as a "team," Connolly, Creamer and Piasecki would present to management their findings and recommendations. As of December 1, 1980, Vidar began to offer full medical, dental, and prorated life insurance and retirement benefits for all part-time employees working 20 hours or more a week.

Benefits to Employer

Recruiting, Retention of Employees. In a competitive industry or area, job sharing is a way to retain workers with valuable experience and training and, as Connolly observes, "it is a more than viable, creative solution to the intense competition for good employees."

Productivity, Efficiency. With combined experience and knowledge, two people in one job can be more productive and more creative in problem solving than a single person, says another Vidar manager. He also lauds the wider range of ability to deal with different people and problems. Creamer and Piasecki note that the pace is more intense in a part-time job, which leads to increased efficiency. Additionally, they believe that burnout is less likely. During 1980, the team was responsible for college recruiting at six schools. By splitting the schedule, each job sharer had less travel, recruiting, and follow-up responsibility. While one was on campus, the other continued to handle the day-to-day activities at the office.

Reduced Absenteeism. The job sharers have had to take almost no personal leave because three is sufficient time outside work hours to attend to personal business. If one sharer must be out, the other can cover. During peak periods, the firm has two trained people to call on to meet the extra workload.

Publicity. Vidar has benefited from nationwide publicity in newspapers, magazines, radio, and television because of its job sharing arrangement.

Perceptions of the Job Sharers

The major advantage cited by Creamer and Piasecki is that job sharing lets them combine the goals of a professional career with the responsibility of family life. They are able to maintain their job skills and are in a position to return more easily to full-time work later. At the same time, they value the time they spend with their children during an important phase of their children's development.

Although the two were prepared to take reduced salaries and benefits, they have encountered some unanticipated problems, including a loss of identity. Supervisors confuse the two. Some prefer dealing with the first person they have contacted. Further, it is difficult for them to advance or transfer to other areas in the Human Resources Department as a team. The sharers perceive the problem to be a result partly of their different skill levels and partly of management's reluctance to enter untried areas.

Requirements for Effective Job Sharing

Company publications about job sharing suggest criteria for setting up a program. Connolly underscores the need for a supportive organizational climate. "Vidar management is committed to the value of the individual," he wrote, "and this helped the arrangement work despite difficulties."

Other requirements include compatibility, communication, job coverage, and commitment. The sharers must be able to get along well and should work out in advance practices that are mutually acceptable. Communications procedures should be established so that information can be transmitted accurately and in a timely manner to each other, supervisors, and co-workers. The schedule should take into account the work demands and staffing needs of the department, and the sharers should be willing to cover for each other when one is out. Finally, the sharers should be committed to the company, their supervisor(s), and each other in order for the team concept to work.

Conclusion

Creamer and Piasecki are currently the only job sharing team at Vidar. However, Connolly says several other managers and employees have expressed interest in job sharing.

While Connolly concedes that job sharing requires additional time and energy, his overall assessment is favorable. "The synergistic effect of the combined effort leads to more productive workers," he says. "For TRW, it was well worth the time and effort!"

JOB SHARING

State of California

The California Employment Development Department (EDD) is the state agency responsible for coordinating public employment services for job seekers and employers. It also administers the claim payment phase of Unemployment Insurance (UI) and Disability Insurance (DI), and the tax collection and accounting functions under the UI, DI, and Personal Income Tax Withholding.

Headquartered in Sacramento, with field offices throughout the state, EDD employs 13,000 to 16,000 persons, depending on the workload. Although state EDD employees currently are not unionized, they have this right under legislation passed in 1979.

Job Sharing Teams

In 1979, the EDD began limited experimentation with job sharing with the development of two job sharing teams in the Sacramento office. One team holds the position of Deputy Director of the Legislative Liaison Office. Responsible for lobbying the California legislature on behalf of the department regarding proposed legislation affecting state government employment services, they supervise a staff of nine employees, five program analysts, and four secretaries.

The other team shares the role of State Supervisor in the Special Applicant Group of the Employment Services Division, and is responsible for three state programs: Job Search Workshops, Federal Food Stamps, and Federal Bonding Programs.

Decisionmaking

In 1979, Mary Davies, who formerly had been Deputy Director of the Legislative Liaison Office, wanted to return to the department on a less than full-time basis after having spent a year working in Washington, D.C. At (then) Director Martin Glick's suggestion, she sought a job sharing partner and approached Elisabeth Kersten, a former legislative employee who recently had left work to be at home with her children. The two worked out a mutually agreeable time schedule where Davies worked three-fifths time and Kersten two-fifths. After discussing the operational issues involved in sharing a job, Kersten and Davies wrote a memo of understanding outlining each person's responsibilities in the job sharing arrangement. (Kersten's background was in budgeting and financial issues; Davies had expertise in the unemployment insurance system.) This was acceptable to Glick and to the Governor's office.

In June 1980, Davies decided to devote all her energy to a new business. Kersten wanted to remain on a part-time basis, but agreed to lengthen her workweek by one day to provide job continuity. Vonnie Madigan, a former legislative aide searching for a job sharing position, was hired to replace Davies. Madigan currently works two days each week.

In Spring 1979, within career civil service channels, Annette Schaffner and Lydia Olivas (with 25 and 20 years of state service respectively) also were exploring the possibility of job sharing. Schaffner was considering retirement but was ambivalent about a total withdrawal from the workforce. She mentioned her interest in working part time to Olivas, who wanted more free time to spend with her family as well as to pursue other activities. Their initial proposal to form a job sharing team met with resistance. When they learned about the other team (one-and-a-half years later), they tried again, and this time their new division chief agreed to their request.

The next step was finding a position and a supervisor willing to accept a job sharing team. The supervisor of the Special Applicant Group, Bill Fly, who had worked with both women, offered them a position in his group of four program analysts. Schaffner, Olivas, and Fly held several meetings to discuss job responsibilities, expectations, and potential problems before the transfer occurred.

Employer Impact

EDD's management has been very pleased with the performance of the job sharers. Says Fly, "I got the best bargain. I get 110 percent from each person while they're on the job. They really want to be at work." Fly adds that virtually no sick leave has been used.

There has been an unanticipated benefit from the arrangements. Occasionally, the Deputy Director must represent EDD's interest at two concurrent hearings on relevant legislation. "Through job sharing, the Deputy Director can be in two places at once," observes Kersten.

The EDD realized another benefit: continuity in the Deputy Director position. First, through retention of Davies and, when she resigned, through the retention of Kersten, the EDD has always had someone available to lobby on the Department's behalf when a staff change occurred. The new employee has had the added benefit of learning the job from an experienced person.

Communication

Job sharers, supervisors, and co-workers agree that job sharing requires more, and better, communication. Both teams emphasize that while the support of supervisors and staff is essential (Schaffner notes that Bill Fly's support was a "crucial factor" in the success of her job sharing arrangement), it is the responsibility of the sharers to devise methods of communication to ensure adequate and accurate transfer of information on the day-to-day status of work activities. Each team devises methods which fit their work patterns. For example, both teams use telephone calls and log books to bring each other current on activities. However, one team finds sharing an office facilitates information transfer while the other believes that separate work space is essential.

More important, both teams have developed work schedules that not only fit their personal lives, but also, they believe, provide the office with flexibility to meet work demands and minimize disruption. Madigan and Kersten divide the workweek according to the workload requirements of the office. Olivas and Schaffner each work two-and-one-half days a week. One works the beginning of the week and the other the last part, with a half-day overlap to discuss their workload.

Training

All job sharers at EDD had prior experience in their positions and did not require formal training. However, as supervisors of programs that frequently change, Schaffner and Olivas occasionally need to attend workshops that provide updated information. Because of a tight travel budget, it is impossible for both to go, so they agreed to send whoever was scheduled to work the day of the workshop.

Fringe Benefits

Under California law, all state employees who work more than 20 hours a week receive the full range of fringe benefits. Health, life, dental, and disability insurance are paid in full; vacation and sick leave are prorated according to the number of hours worked.

The salary of the Deputy Director, an appointed position, is fixed. After one year of experimenting with the job sharing arrangement, the department's evaluation division conducted a formal evaluation and concluded that the arrangement was operating effectively.

For civil servants, the issues of promotion and job evaluation were somewhat different. Fly had supervised both Olivas and Schaffner before they became a team; since he knew their performance capabilities, evaluation was not perceived as a difficulty. Promotion was a moot issue. A few months prior to beginning their job sharing assignment, both women had received a promotion. Because of their years of service and the reduced work hours, both realized that future promotions might take longer despite good performance appraisals. However, they were more interested in balancing their work and personal lives and were willing to trade increased income for more non-worktime.

Problems

According to Fly, job sharing not only requires supervisors to spend more time on communications, but also involves supervisors more closely in the day-to-day work of the job sharers. While Fly believes that this extra administrative burden on the supervisor is an issue those who advocate job sharing must acknowledge, he is quick to point out that the benefits accruing from job sharing far make up for the effort.

For the Legislative Liaison Office, the management aspect has caused some difficulties. Some subordinates, for example, find reporting to two people burdensome; they feel they often have to repeat the same information twice. A more serious issue is the lack of opportunity staff perceive for the informal exchange of information that often accompanies professional positions. Because of their reduced hours, Kersten and Madigan concentrate more on tasks and spend less time on the intangible, social aspect of office functioning. To partially resolve these problems, their full-time assistant serves as the focal point for channelling information, solving problems, and coordinating day-to-day operations and acts as an intermediary between staff and the Deputy Director.

Employee Impact

All the EDD job sharers find the reduced work hours personally satisfying and well worth the extra effort.

According to Kersten, job sharers in professionally demanding positions, like their full-time counterparts, are subject to pressures to work extra hours. Kersten believes job sharers must learn to set realistic limits on the amount of work they can accomplish in their normal work schedules. This requires not only efficient work habits, but also the ability to determine priorities.

JOB SHARING

The Black and Decker
Manufacturing Company

Started in 1910 as a small, specialty machinery shop by S. Duncan Black and Alonzo G. Decker, the Black and Decker Manufacturing Company (B&D) is now the world's leading manufacturer and marketer of portable power tools, with sales of $1.4 billion in 1980. Sales and earnings have increased nearly 20 times in the 20 years between 1960 and 1980. Headquarters are located at Towson, Maryland.

Decisionmaking

"It's an interesting concept. Let's give it a try," was the attitude of B&D Personnel Manager John Shobert when approached in 1979 by an area college to participate in a special job sharing internship program. Under the Women's Management Development Project at Goucher College in Towson, Black & Decker (as well as other area businesses) was asked to employ a job sharing team for 13 weeks in order to provide training and work experience to college-educated women who had been out of the workforce, serving in volunteer capacities, or devoting their time to family activities for a number of years. The team was compensated, but employers were not obligated to hire the women as permanent employees at the end of the internship.

Black & Decker had never considered job sharing, but management thought the program offered a way to learn more about job sharing and, at the same time, to respond to community needs.

Shobert hired two women to share the job of Personnel Specialist. The job sharing arrangement worked out so well that both members were hired on a permanent basis in that position. The company also took an additional two interns from the next Goucher class. However, these interns worked on a part-time basis (20 hours per week) in two separate areas, Accounting and Management Information Systems, and did not share a job. Both subsequently have been hired on a full-time basis.

Company Considerations

Some of the issues considered by Black & Decker and the way they were handled were:

- Identifying positions for job sharing. Shobert identified the job of Personnel Specialist as appropriate to job sharing. Since the work is project oriented and each project has a beginning and an end, the job sharers can work fairly independently of each other and others in the personnel department.

- Choosing the team. Goucher's program tries to ensure a workable match. When the internship worked out well, Shobert offered the position on a permanent basis to the two interns. One decided that she wasn't yet ready to take a permanent job, so Shobert asked Goucher to recommend candidates who had completed the program and then relied heavily on the remaining job sharer's evaluation of the candidate for final selection for the position. He believes successful job sharing is more likely when a good relationship exists between the sharers.

- Scheduling. Both job sharers work two-and-a-half days a week (20 hours). One works Monday and Tuesday; the other Thursday and Friday, with both working an overlap of a half day on Wednesday.

- Communication. Job sharing requires planned communication between the job sharers themselves and with their supervisor, and between the job sharers and co-workers, Shobert observes. During the internship, there was also communication with Goucher College.

  The job sharers communicate daily by telephone and at crossover time each Wednesday. Further, they maintain careful logs about work accomplished and outstanding. Departmental staff meetings are scheduled for Wednesdays so that both job sharers can be present. As their supervisor, Shobert talks to each job sharer separately concerning individual assignments and jointly about job-shared projects.

- Fringe Benefits. Each job sharer is eligible for the same benefits as full-time workers, but on a prorated basis, according to time worked. An exception is medical benefits, which are fully covered by Black & Decker.

Shobert notes that job sharing adds only a minimal cost to the company. In addition to the medical benefit, the company pays Maryland's workers' compensation and social security taxes for both sharers.

- Productivity. Shobert notes first that the job sharers are task oriented, then adds that they are very enthusiastic and maintain a high energy level. However, he cautions that he can't compare productivity to full-timers in the job, since the position was newly created. An aspect of job sharing that he particularly likes is that each sharer brings strengths to the job. On the Personnel Specialist team, for example, one member has special skills in writing and speaking; the other excells at organization and administration.

- Promotions and Merit Increases. The job sharers are eligible for merit pay increases and are rated separately based on their individual effort, as well as on the results of group projects. They may apply for any permanent full-time job and are considered for those jobs as would any other worker. However, the shared Personnel Specialist position will remain at the same level of responsibility for each job sharer.

- Job Satisfaction. Both women are well satisfied with the job sharing arrangement. It gives them time for their families (each has young children), time for community volunteer activities (in which both are heavily involved), and the opportunity to prepare for the transition to full-time work.

Both women have undergraduate degrees and one has a graduate degree; both had worked prior to raising a family.

- Limitations. Shobert thinks there would be problems in sharing a job for which tasks were not discrete or which required continuity. Most higher rated managerial positions could be handled better by one permanent part-time worker, he believes.

Conclusions

Shobert points out some criteria for success in job sharing: planning activities in advance, ensuring that a good relationship exists between sharers, and setting out the ground rules—particularly on promotions—at the outset. (For example, if either Personnel Specialist job sharer wishes to be considered for a job with more responsibility, she has the same rights as full-time workers in applying, but could no longer be a job sharer.) Given this, job sharing benefits the company by bringing the complementary skills of two workers to one position and, at the same time, serves the needs of certain groups of workers in the community.

EXTENDED HOLIDAYS

General Motors, Ford Motor Company, United Auto Workers

Over the years, the United Auto Workers (UAW), General Motors (GM), and Ford have negotiated a growing package of paid time off for most workers in these two firms. Approximately 496,000 UAW-represented employees at GM and 150,000 UAW-represented employees at Ford were covered by the agreements, effective October 1979, which specified annual paid time off for UAW members as follows:

Vacation (with 20 years of service)	20 days
Excused Absence Allowance (may be scheduled as vacation)	5 days
Holidays	13-15 days
Paid Personal Holidays	8-9 days

Vacations generally are scheduled in 1-week increments. Scheduling arrangements range from a plant shutdown, at which time all or most employees take their vacations, to individual vacations approved by department supervisors. In the event of scheduling conflicts between employees, plant seniority generally prevails. UAW members may have the option, or occasionally the requirement, of working instead of taking earned vacation days. In these instances, employees receive the equivalent of two days pay for each vacation day worked, in addition to any other applicable premiums.

The paid absence allowance permits workers to use five days of paid leave in increments of not less than four hours. It is designed to allow workers to attend to personal matters such as doctor and dental appointments without losing a full day's wages, or it may be used as additional vacation.

The number of paid holidays is stated as a range because the length of the Christmas holiday period varies from six to eight days, depending on the day of the week on which Christmas and New Years fall.

Paid Personal Holidays (PPH) are the most recent addition to the package of paid time off. It was first negotiated in the 1976 contract, providing 12 days over the last two years of that contract. The plan was extended in the 1979 GM and Ford agreements to provide 26 days over a 3-year period—8 days the first year and 9 days each of the last two years.

Ford and GM assign each worker to scheduling numbers that provide one day off at a time at reasonably predictable intervals. Assignments and schedules are computerized and drawn up well in advance, enabling employees as well as management to plan for PPH days.

Mondays, Fridays, and days before and after holidays are considered preferred days. PPH days are not scheduled according to seniority and management distributes preferred days on an equitable basis. To receive pay for an assigned day off, the worker must have worked both the preceding and suceeding scheduled working days. Furthermore, an employee is not permitted to work on a PPH day, except in an emergency situation. Employees with less than one year of service are ineligible for PPH.

The impetus for PPH grew out of heavy overtime in 1973 and 1976, going into and coming out of the 1974-75 recession, according to UAW researcher Dan Luria.* Many UAW workers were on extended layoffs during the recession. As the economy began to improve in 1975, the auto manufacturers met increased demand through extensive overtime. Laid off workers were recalled slowly as the companies became confident that the upswing would continue. The UAW was faced with a political issue: how should the conflicting conditions of many layoffs and much overtime be reconciled, especially in light of UAW's philosophy strongly favoring job creation through such approaches as worktime reduction and early retirement? Thus, one of the major UAW issues in the 1976 negotiations was job security. Accordingly, one of the purposes of PPH, as stated in the agreement, is to provide additional job opportunities.

---

*Victor Leo of Ford and F.R. Curd, Jr. of General Motors also contributed to this case study.

Job Creation

Although Ford and GM officials say it is difficult to calculate a specific number of jobs that have been created, there is little doubt that employment opportunities have increased due to PPH. According to these officials, job creation is less likely in areas other than assembly line jobs—material handlers, tool and die makers, etc.—where careful work scheduling and preparation can compensate for workers on a paid personal holiday, thus minimizing the need for additional employees. In contrast, for the closely coordinated and integrated assembly line operations, where every position must be filled at all times, additional workers are needed to fill any absences—paid or unpaid, excused, or unexcused. Luria estimates that 20,000 jobs, in all categories, have been created. He derives this figure from the 1979 base of 650,000 U.S. hourly employees (Ford and GM combined), deducting the eight paid personal holidays per year, and incorporating a 0.85 factor that reflects less than a one-to-one replacement rate.

Company Concerns

From the companies' perspective, the important issues are full and efficient utilization of facilities and equipment and maintenance of product quality. Achieving these objectives depends to a certain extent on their ability to schedule the workforce. Officials from both corporations note that as long as plant management knows sufficiently in advance which employees will be working on a given day, it can generally make preparations to ensure full utilization of facilities and equipment. Therefore, the contract vests scheduling of PPH days in the hands of the company.

The companies' experience does not show that additional contractual paid time off has resulted in a decrease in absenteeism. The increase in absenteeism is baffling to both management and the UAW. Luria suggests that some workers may be making time-money trade-offs between the paid time off—which cannot always be taken off—and unpaid, self-timed AWOL (i.e., unexcused) absences for the purpose of enhancing the quality of their lives. Supporting this contention is the fact that at GM only about 50 percent of earned vacation days are actually used. A GM official also suggested that one reason for increased AWOL may be the reduction of mini-layoffs for model changes. These layoffs, from a few days up to six weeks, were more prevalent in the early 1970s. With Supplemental Unemployment Benefits (SUB) providing many workers with nearly full take-home pay when laid off, workers may have used that time off to satisfy vacation needs. As mini-layoffs become less prevalent, the GM official suggests some workers may be meeting their vacation needs through increased AWOL absences.

Regardless of the reasons behind the absences, the UAW and the auto companies acknowledge that unexcused absences create production inefficiencies. Unplanned-for absences cause plant disruptions, especially at the start of the shift when plant managers and supervisors must quickly reassign personnel to ensure that all assembly line posts are filled. Additional permanent and part-time personnel have to be hired to accommodate AWOLs. On days when absences are low (payday, for example), plants are burdened with extra workers, adding to operating costs. When this occurs, ironically, some supervisors may seek volunteers willing to take a day off without pay to minimize excess-worker costs.

The UAW jointly with GM and Ford is addressing the problem through their respective joint labor-management committees established for the purpose of developing new concepts and pilot projects which encourage voluntary employee participation in identifying and solving work-related problems. In addition, their efforts are directed at minimizing the disruptive effects of unwarranted absenteeism, improving product quality, and examining alternative work schedules designed to improve the work climate and increase the utilization of facilities. At Ford, the labor-management committee is called the National Joint Committee on Employe Involvement. At GM, the parties negotiated a memorandum of understanding on attendance in 1979 negotiations, providing for the establishment of a joint labor-management National Committee on Attendance to develop programs directed at reducing unwarranted absences. In addition, GM and the UAW have established a Committee to Improve the Quality of Work Life, responsible for exploring and undertaking projects to improve the work environment of employees represented by the UAW.

EXTENDED VACATION

United Steelworkers of America*

In agreement with the Amalgamated Association of Iron, Steel and Tin Workers (founded in 1876), a massive organizing drive throughout the steel industry was launched in 1936 under the sponsorship of the Congress of Industrial Organizations (CIO). Membership growth and collective bargaining progress led to the formation in 1942 of the United Steelworkers of America (USWA). USWA continued to grow through mergers with four other unions between 1944 and 1972. Currently, its membership totals approximately 1,400,000 in 5,200 affiliated local unions through the United States, Canada, Puerto Rico, and the Virgin Islands. Members are production, maintenance, clerical, technical, and plant-protection workers employed primarily in the basic steel and allied ferrous and nonferrous metals producing and fabricating industries.

As outlined in an official pamphlet, USWA's philosophy states, in part: "The Steelworkers maintain that full employment is a realistic and necessary condition in the Nation. . . . The Union also seeks a shorter work week or shorter work year as an important part of its program to promote full employment and job security." Toward its objectives of full employment and job security, USWA has negotiated a reduction of worktime for its members, including retirement on full pension after 30 years of service regardless of age, and the Extended Vacation (EV) program.

Extended Vacation Benefit Agreement

According to James R. Thomas of USWA's Contract Department, the Steelworkers negotiated an extended vacation benefit rather than other worktime reduction approaches, such as shorter workdays, shorter workweeks, or periodic days off,

---

*The information for this case study was obtained primarily from the union representatives.

because the latter approaches are impractical for the steel industry's continuous manufacturing process.

The USWA extended vacation benefit is similar to the Australian steel industry's program which provides each worker 13 weeks vacation every five years, enabling the many English-born Australian steelworkers to return to England for visits. The program was described to USWA by an Australian steelworker delegate to a USWA conference in the early 1960s.

USWA pursued the idea and in 1962 negotiated an extended vacation benefit for its 450,000 members in the steel industry. The current 5-year program cycle, which began January 1, 1979 and runs through December 31, 1983, operates as follows:

- Once every five years, the workforce in each plant is separated into two groups on the basis of seniority, creating the "Senior EV" and "Junior EV" groups.

- Each group is further divided into five sections on the basis of seniority; 20 percent of the most senior employees in the Senior EV group are assigned to take their extended vacation during the first year of the 5-year cycle. Succeeding sections of 20 percent are assigned subsequent years, until the 5-year cycle is completed.

- Extended vacation benefits:

  1. Senior EV employees are eligible for a total of 13 weeks (14 if over 25 years' service) paid vacation during the assigned benefit year. The EV subsumes the regular vacation period (5 weeks for an employee with 25 or more years of service; 4 weeks for 17-24 years of service; 3 weeks for 10-16 years of service). In other words, an employee in the Senior EV group gets an additional vacation of either 9 or 10 weeks during the benefit year.

  2. Junior EV employees are eligible for 4 weeks of the extended vacation benefit in addition to the regular vacation period. An employee with 1-2 years of service earns 1 week of regular vacation, while those with 3-9 years of service get 2 weeks. Therefore, during the EV benefit year, vacation for employees in the junior group totals 5-6 weeks.

- Extended vacation scheduling options:

1. Originally, all of the 13 weeks of extended vacation had to be taken consecutively. In subsequent agreements, USWA negotiated a more flexible arrangement for members who desire more money and less time off (the concerns of Junior EV's are described in the Evaluation section). An employee now may reduce the extended vacation by up to 3 weeks and receive cash in lieu of time off.

2. A further modification allows employees to split the extended vacation into two different years.

USWA also has negotiated EV benefits for its 85,000 members in the aluminum industries, but in a slightly different form. In the aluminum industry, there are no senior and junior groups. Everyone with at least three years of service is given 10 weeks off and paid for 13 weeks, once every five years. In the can industry, the senior group is comprised of everyone with at least 15 years' seniority, and the plan is otherwise similar to Basic Steel.

Evaluation

Although EV does increase employment opportunities, according to James Thomas of the Contract Department, USWA officials cannot cite specific figures. They do, however, rule out a 1-to-1 replacement rate. One reason is the change in their own policy to negotiate a reduced extended vacation period allowing members to work additional days for the purpose of earning extra money. Another important factor cited is the resourcefulness of plant managers. To keep costs down, plant managers first attempt to pick up the slack through rescheduling and overtime; they hire additional workers only as a last resort.

Thomas noted some problems associated with extended vacations. Splitting the workforce in the steel industry into senior and junior groups with dramatically unequal benefits has created the appearance of first- and second-class members. There are complaints when a member misses getting into the senior group by a few weeks of seniority. Notwithstanding the complaints, the membership has voted overwhelmingly to continue the existing plan each negotiating session. As noted, USWA avoided this problem in the aluminum industry by negotiating the same EV benefit for all employees.

Another problem area is scheduling EV. Many junior employees are assigned an EV period during the school months, when vacation options are limited.

Use of Extended Vacation

Although there are no recent studies analyzing what members do during EV, a study commissioned in the mid-1960s showed that workers used their EV for vacation rather than moonlighting. The study also noted that groups of workers shared in the expense of purchasing recreation vehicles to be used in turn by each member of the group as their EV assigned dates came around. Thomas said that judging by the postcards received at headquarters, many members travel abroad. With a large segment of the membership being second and third generation eastern Europeans, the EV benefit enables many of them to visit their ancestral homes.

3
FLEXIBLE WORKLIFE OPTIONS

This chapter covers three new work scheduling arrangements—voluntary time-income trade-offs, leaves (sabbaticals and social service leaves), and flexible retirement. While the arrangements discussed in previous chapters contribute to flexible worklives, these three are distinct approaches. They are, in effect, arrangements developed by employers to provide periodic breaks in worklives for full-time employees who meet certain requirements.

As in all other work hour reduction arrangements, the implementing organization expects net gains (i.e., retaining skilled employees, enhancing corporate image). However, in flexible worklife options the element of social responsibility is a significant factor.

Voluntary Time-Income Trade-Offs

Voluntary time-income trade-off arrangements provide an opportunity for full-time employees to voluntarily reduce their wages or salaries for additional time off work. The option is renewable at predetermined intervals, providing flexibility for both the organization and employees.

Our research reveals that concern about layoffs resulting from budget cuts or recession has stimulated creation of trade-off arrangements. For example, management at Ticor Title Insurers, Realty Tax and Service Division, did not want to lose trained personnel when sales were down during Spring 1979; they were concerned that such losses were difficult to absorb in the small offices they operated. Employees felt solidarity toward each other. Rather than see junior employees laid off, 12 employees in three southern California Realty Tax offices volunteered to reduce their workweeks from 40 hours to 32 hours for 90 days. Similar voluntary cutbacks were tried successfully later in three other California Realty Tax offices.

While in several instances this type of innovation was developed in response to deteriorating economic conditions, we found that in some cases the programs provided secondary, and often positive, outcomes for the organization and its employees. Because of these benefits, some organizations subsequently have made the programs a part of their organization's personnel policy and have adapted the arrangements to the changing needs of the organization and the employees.

Employee decisions about time-income trade-offs appear to be based on a number of factors: employees may be more likely to exchange income for time when they are concerned about layoffs, if they have personal needs for additional time, or if the option is available at certain times of the year.

A report titled "Exchanging Earnings for Leisure" examined the findings of a national survey conducted in August 1978 by Louis Harris & Associates. Prepared by Fred Best for the U.S. Department of Labor and the National Commission for Employment Policy, the report revealed that prevailing worktime conditions are at variance with the preferences of many workers. Many workers indicated a clear preference for extended periods away from work—that is, longer vacations and sabbaticals—over shorter-range gains such as reduced workdays or workweeks. The report concludes that the way in which potential gains in free time are scheduled is a major determinant of whether individuals are willing to trade earnings for time.

An earlier survey by J. Brad Chapman and Robert Otterman[1] analyzed worker preferences for various forms of compensation and benefit options. The findings indicate a strong employee desire for extra vacation but little demand for shorter workdays. (The order of preference was extra vacation first, followed by pay increases, pension increases, family dental benefits, early retirement, the 4-day workweek, and shorter workdays.) Those surveyed who were younger than 35 and older than 50 clearly preferred extra vacations, while workers in the 36 to 49 year age group ranked higher pay as a first priority.

Legislation, S.B. 1859, The Reduced Worktime Act, was adopted in California last year (Chapter 817, Statute 80, approved by the Governor in July 1980) to allow most state employees to choose reduced work schedules with comparable reductions in pay. Existing California law (Chapter 938, Statute 79, signed by the Governor September 1979) permits employees to voluntarily reduce their worktime in state agencies and departments contemplating a reduction in personnel equivalent to 1 percent or more of full-time equivalent jobs. California also enacted into law (Chapter 751, Statute 79, approved by the Governor September 1979) an experimental leisure sharing program aimed at job creation in the private sector. Under this program, employees can voluntarily reduce their hours of work and their employers could hire additional employees to keep production at the same level. Grants can be made to participating employers to offset increases in labor costs, but no funds were appropriated. Employees choosing to reduce their worktime would be given first priority to return to full time if they desired.

---

1. J. Brad Chapman and Robert Otterman, "Employees' Preferences for Various compensation and Fringe Benefit Options," *The Personnel Administrator,* November 1975.

Leaves

Leaves generally fit into two categories. One is *sabbaticals*—paid blocks of time away from work to pursue leisure or personal interests. The second is *social service leave*—paid time away from the workplace to assist non-profit agencies. Generally, leaves are work arrangements that provide additional time away from work to individuals who have been employed by a particular firm for a length of time.

1. *Sabbaticals* have long been part of the university scene and therefore faculty sabbaticals are not included in the case studies. They have only recently been adopted by corporations and government.

Employers offer sabbaticals for various reasons. One is to prevent employee burnout in competitive, achievement-oriented environments where long hours are often required. Another is to make employment more attractive, to both prospective and current employees, by making sabbaticals part of the fringe benefit package.

All examples we uncovered have service requirements. Some sabbaticals are one-time-only options, while others become available again after a certain number of additional service years. Leave time often can be attached to regular vacation. While some sabbaticals are automatic, others require employees to submit applications, the procedure depending largely on the objective of the arrangement. In no instance could employees exchange time off for pay; nor could they work elsewhere in paid employment.

Tandem Computers, Inc., a computer firm in California's Silicon Valley, offers all employees a 6-week sabbatical, in addition to annual vacation, every four years. Begun in 1974, the company has grown rapidly in a highly competitive industry. Tandem's president and co-founder James G. Treybig believes the company's people-oriented management style is a major factor in the company's success. According to Treybig, the company developed the sabbatical as another expression of its commitment to its employees.

Time-Life Books, now headquartered in Alexandria, Virginia, has changed its sabbatical program to better accommodate worker needs. When the plan was put into effect in 1968, it allowed employees who had 20 years of continuous service to take six months of leave (or two separate 3-month blocks) at half salary. Some years later, the service requirement was reduced to 15 years. Because many employees said they couldn't afford to reduce their salaries by half, the program was further revised in 1978 so that employees with 20 years of service can elect three months off at 75 percent of their regular salaries. Vice President of Personnel Beatrice T. Dobie reports that no figures on the extent of usage have been kept, but estimates that a dozen workers have taken advantage of the program. She views it as a benefit for "long-term employees whom we value. The sabbatical is a refresher."

In developing the Civil Service Reform Act (which became law in 1978) federal researchers studied and adapted a number of personnel policies from the private sector and universities, one of which was a sabbatical approach. Long term civil service employees with two years of career Senior Executive Service (a category introduced in the 1978 Act) are eligible for a paid sabbatical, with continuing fringe benefits, of up to 11 months. Those eligible can take one sabbatical in any 10-year period, provided the proposal they submit is approved. The intent is for development and enrichment of employees. They are prohibited from taking sabbaticals if they are eligible for retirement, and they must have held executive type positions for a minimum of seven years. The first sabbaticals will begin late in 1981 and it is expected that only a handful of employees will meet eligibility requirements in the early years of the program.

2. In *social service leave,* the motivation is to stimulate employee involvement in the community by allowing an employee time off to work at a social service organization while providing full pay, full benefits, and a guarantee of reentry at the same grade, responsibility, and status.

In the examples of social service leave we uncovered, employees were required to submit proposals clearly defining their project goals and identifying groups with which they proposed to work. Usually special committees formed by the companies evaluate the applications and, occasionally, provide follow-up.

Since 1971, International Business Machines (IBM), headquartered in Armonk, New York, has encouraged full-time employees to take up to one year's paid absence to work with community organizations. IBM gives consideration to service assignments that are initiated by interested agencies, the company itself, or by IBM employees. Program Manager John C. Steers says the program was initiated for the dual purpose of assisting nonprofit organizations and supporting employee involvement in the community, and in this way fulfilling the company's responsibilities to be "a good corporate citizen." Between 1971 and 1979, more than 500 employees participated.

Public Policy Recommendations on Leaves

In 1977, Jule Sugarman, former Deputy Director of the Office of Personnel Management, prepared a paper for the National Conference on Alternative Work Schedules (sponsored by the National Council for Alternative Work Patterns) outlining a "decennial sabbatical" plan. The plan (which he later revised and presented during the California

State Senate's November 1977 hearings on "Leisure Sharing") provides for a percentage of an individual's earnings and/or an employer contribution to be set aside so that over a period of nine years sufficient funds are accrued to finance a tenth year of nonwork. Sugarman's major objective is to provide employment opportunities; he does not, however, expect a replacement rate of 1-to-1. His plan provides a way to "systematically remove individuals from the labor market for certain portions of their working lives," which Sugarman believes is possible only with a system of compensation. Additionally, Sugarman sees the time off as a chance for people to continue their education or participate in voluntary community service.

During the 95th Congress, 2nd Session, Senator Donald W. Riegle, Jr. (D-MI) introduced the Education and Child Care Reemployment Rights Act (S. 2485), which would allow any worker in private industry who has worked with an organization for more than five years to request up to five years' absence with the right of returning to a job at the same level, content, and pay. No action was taken on the bill by the Senate Committee on Human Resources. Senator Riegle plans to introduce a modified version of his bill. He regards this as an innovative and timely subject that should be considered and discussed by the Congress.

Phased Retirement

Phased retirement (also called gradual, flexible, or transition retirement) is a gradual reduction of work hours for older employees prior to full retirement. Our examination shows that phased retirement programs fall into two general categories: reduced workweek and reduced workyear. In a reduced workweek program, employees meeting eligibility requirements can reduce workweeks to four or three days, often on a graduated basis; a reduction in hours worked may be accompanied by a reduction in salary. In a reduced workyear, employees who meet service and/or age requirements may take off blocks of time, either as extended leave or vacation.

Length of leave sometimes is tied to age and/or length of service. Leave may be paid or unpaid, though participation in an unpaid program is voluntary. Depending on management philosophy, program objectives, and collective bargaining agreements, there may be restrictions on the use of leave (e.g., leave must be taken in blocks; leave may or may not be exchanged for lump sum payments).

Because of management and employee concerns that reduced incomes due to reductions in worktime during the years preceding retirement may result in reduced retirement benefits, some organizations have annualized the salaries of employees participating in flexible retirement programs for purposes of computing retirement benefits. Fringe benefits generally are fully maintained in reduced workyear programs, but are often prorated in reduced workweek arrangements.

Some companies view phased retirement as a means of retaining skilled older workers and reducing pension costs at the same time. According to the Winter 1979 issue of *Aging and Work,* Teledyne Continental Motors of Milwaukee began its "Golden Bridges" program when company officials found that 50 percent of their workforce had more than 25 years of service and that the flow of talented employees into retirement was depriving the company of much of its skilled workforce. Moreover, retirement benefits were costly. Under "Golden Bridges," workers reaching age 58 with 30 years service receive extra paid vacation, additional life insurance, and increased pension benefits each year they continue working.

Some companies introduce phased retirement, in part, as an incentive for early retirement in order to create jobs. Others maintain that such programs provide a mechanism for training replacements. The rationale for instituting a phased retirement program often reflects the particular labor market facing the firm or industry.

Most programs are characterized by a desire to help workers prepare for retirement—essentially to ease the transition from work to retirement. Many managers, particularly those involved in retirement policy, believe that even with preretirement counseling, employees often are surprised when they experience difficulties dealing with unstructured time. In response, companies have designed phased retirement programs to provide the experience of retirement, rather than just information about it.

Application in Some American Companies

That is the reason Towle Silversmiths, Inc. of Newburyport, Massachusetts has, since the 1940s, offered forty days off during the four months prior to retirement for employees who retire at age 65. Originally initiated by Towle Company and later included in Towle's contract with the International Jewelry Workers, employees receive one day off a week with pay during the first month, two days off the second, and so on.

Mutual of New York offers all employees aged 55 with 10 years of service one paid day off a week for the 52 weeks preceding planned retirement. The Preretirement Leave program is offered as a one-time-only option. Workers may elect to take off any day of the week (worked out with their supervisor), but they are encouraged to take Mondays or Fridays off to get used to the extra unstructured free time. According to William Doherty, Supervisor of the Benefits Section, Human Resources Department, the response of older workers has been enthusiastic since the program was initiated many years ago (it was then affectionately called "hobby lobby days"), with full participation by eligible workers. About 20 to 25 employees are eligible each year.

New England Mutual Life Insurance Company of Boston also is concerned about preparing its employees for retirement. Before the passage of the Age Discrimination in Employment Amendments, employees with 10 years of service had been eligible to receive two additional weeks of paid vacation during the year of their 62nd birthday, with increments of one week for the next two years. This policy is under review due to the elimination of mandatory retirement at age 65.

Also reflecting a concern for its long-time employees, Ideal Industries of Sycamore, Illinois (chapter 2 includes a case study of a shorter workweek program at Ideal) provides extended paid leave to employees who have 30 years service. Beginning with their 30th anniversary with the company, and every 5th anniversary thereafter, salaried and hourly employees are eligible for a 2-month paid vacation. Five to ten employees become eligible each year. The leave must be taken during the calendar year of the anniversary and cannot be exchanged for pay. While scheduling of the leave must be worked out with supervisors, personnel policy requires that the leave be taken in at least 1-week increments.

In other years, the length of the employee's paid vacation time reverts to the normal one month. Thus, an employee with 31 years of service who would have received the eight weeks paid vacation the previous year, now would receive four weeks of paid vacation.

About 100 of the 12,000 employees at Polaroid Corporation headquarters in Cambridge, Massachusetts retire each year. The company is experimenting with two types of flexible retirement. The Rehearsal Retirement Plan allows employees preparing for retirement (no age limitation and only one year of service is required) to take a leave of absence of about three months while their jobs are held for them. The Tapering Off Program permits employees to reduce their work hours in a variety of ways (e.g., working shorter days, shorter weeks, or fewer weeks per month) for a few months, and occasionally for as long as three to five years. For purposes of computing pensions, which are based on final average salaries, the reduced salaries are annualized to approximately the full-time equivalent.

The options are individually negotiated, providing flexibility for the company and employees. "Designing a program to meet the employee's and the department's needs," says Joseph Perkins, Corporate Retirement Administrator, "is a very important factor." Perkins notes that supervisors are not as resistant to the arrangements as the company expected.

The Polaroid programs are available to employees at all levels, and eligible employees in a wide range of occupations have taken advantage of them. There has been greater (and increasing) interest in the Tapering Off approach. About half the employees who have taken advantage of Rehearsal Retirement have chosen to retire; the other half have returned to work. Participation in the Rehearsal program may be lower, Perkins believes, because many employees do not see the need to prepare for leisure time. Through preretirement counseling activities, Perkins has learned that many employees believe they will be able to fill their free time easily and do not feel the need to "test the waters."

The European Experience

Phased retirement approaches have been in existence for some time in a number of European countries, including

Belgium, France, Great Britain, the Netherlands, Sweden, West Germany, and Switzerland. These phased retirement programs are typically initiated by top-level management within individual companies out of concern for their older workers. Several unions in the United Kingdom and Federal Republic of Germany have negotiated or are now encouraging such plans as part of collective bargaining agreements.

A nationwide policy was started in Sweden in 1976 that provides a partial pension to workers aged 60 and older as they reduce worktime. Under the Swedish "partial pension scheme," workers aged 60 to 65 who wish to qualify for a partial pension must reduce their working time by at least five hours per week on average and continue working a minimum of 17 hours a week. The pension currently replaces 50 percent (formerly 65 percent) of the income lost through reduced worktime. Thus, a worker's total income from the partial pension and part-time work amounts to 85 percent to 95 percent of income from full-time work. By Spring 1980, a quarter of the 200,000 persons eligible each year were participating in the program. The majority of participants have reduced their work hours from full time to half time. Managers try to schedule these workers either on a half-day basis or full time in alternative weeks, with two persons sharing the same job whenever possible.

The program in Sweden was not started as a means of reducing unemployment. However, when later faced with economic downturns, the use of partial pensions helped to avoid layoffs. Workplaces showing the highest utilization of partial pension tend to be privately owned and in the manufacturing sector, and thus more subject to cyclical fluctuations in the economy.

An extensive study soon to be completed by the National Council for Alternative Work Patterns (NCAWP) explores the development, administration, costs, and benefits of 13 phased retirement programs in Europe.[2] Preliminary conclusions indicate that while phased retirement programs have not been used to force older workers out of the labor force prematurely, neither have they served to extend the working life of employees beyond "normal retirement age" or the age of pension eligibility. Most programs are voluntary for all firm employees, provided that age and service requirements are met. In most European countries and companies included in the study, mandatory retirement at age 65, or earlier, is still the rule.

Study findings also indicate that reduced work schedules have not resulted in severe scheduling problems for supervisors. Indeed, the programs often result in more effective operations, as managers' skills improve in planning work assignments. Absences due to phased retirement are usually known in advance—in some cases, as long as one year ahead of time.

The financial costs of phased retirement programs are viewed as low by many of the participating companies in the NCAWP study. In many programs, participants continue to receive full wages or salary, and experience no loss in fringe benefits or pension credits and contributions. While the current number of participants relative to the size of the company's total workforce is usually small, even the prospects of an increased number of employees phasing into retirement under such schemes does not appear to alarm company executives, although few have collected hard data. The programs are viewed as socially responsible, low cost/high benefit policies. Another benefit results when companies utilize phased retirement programs as a vehicle for training and gradually transferring job responsibility to other employees.

2. Constance Swank, *Case Studies on Phased Retirement: The European Experience,* Washington: National Council for Alternative Work Patterns, 1981.

According to the study findings, managers, employees, and labor union representatives involved in phased retirement programs in Europe express unanimity in their general support of these programs. The problems in implementation and administration of such plans appear to be relatively minor for employers, and the benefits to employees, while not entirely measurable, are nonetheless considerable.

Older Workers' Interest in Reduced Hours of Work

A 1979 Harris poll indicated that fewer workers want to retire early and that many would prefer to retire later. Approximately 46 percent of the retirees polled would prefer to be working. Of those interviewed who were currently employed, half said they would like to continue working; of that 50 percent, nearly one out of four (24 percent) preferred to work part time.

When the State of Wisconsin conducted its pilot program on job sharing (see chapter 2, Project JOIN case study), a number of state employees nearing retirement expressed interest in part-time work. Of the sample group studied, those younger than 65 preferred full-time work (41 percent) to part-time work (29 percent). However, after age 65, only 25 percent still desired full-time work while 14 percent wanted full retirement, 42 percent preferred part-time work, and 19 percent wanted to become part of a resource pool made up of workers available for call back for seasonal jobs, consulting, or special task force employment.

A recent study by the Ethel Percy Andrus Gerontology Center of the University of Southern California analyzed the interest in and feasibility of flexible retirement options.[3] The

---

3. Stephen R. McConnell, Dorothy Fleisher, Carolyn E. Usher, and Barbara Hade Kaplan, *Alternative Work Options for Older Workers: A Feasibility Study,* The Ethel Percy Andrus Gerontology Center, University of Southern California, 1980.

study indicated that managers and union representatives in two locations (a west coast aerospace firm and a city government) underestimated older workers' interest in reduced work hour arrangements.

This interest in worktime reduction was confirmed in a recent survey by Yitzchak Shkop at the University of Illinois.[4] Blue-collar workers and managers approaching retirement at four large northeastern industrial companies were asked to indicate their preferences for employment options—including job and time modification—which might encourage them to extend their worklives. Nearly 75 percent of the 393 respondents who indicated a preference for remaining in the organization wanted to alter the amount of time they worked, either working fewer hours per week or extending their vacations. Of those with preferences for reduced work hour schedules, 42.3 percent of blue-collar workers preferred shorter workdays in a standard week. Managers, on the other hand, preferred (64 percent) a shorter workweek; only 17 percent chose the shorter day option. There was no significant difference between blue-collar workers and managers in selecting longer vacations (approximately 67 percent for each group).

Shkop recommends that organizations give serious consideration to offering a wide range of options (scheduling and job modifications) as a way to prevent the loss of valuable human resources and to prepare for a projected shorter supply of younger workers as well as present and projected shortages of skilled labor.

Reasons for Limited American Experience

Our research reveals that implementation of phased retirement programs is limited in this country, despite an increas-

---

4. *The Effect of Providing Various Options for Continued Employment in the Organization on Patterns of Retirement Plans,* conducted under a grant from the National Commission on Employment Policy, U.S. Department of Labor, forthcoming 1981.

ing number of recommendations for expanded flexible retirement options. Few organizations in America have started programs because of a lack of role models and a paucity of operational, administrative, and compensation information. Where these programs have been adopted, participation by eligible employees is low and participants often do not take all the leave available to them.

A number of reasons may account for low employee participation or underutilization of leave. In addition to not feeling a need to prepare for retirement, older workers are concerned about reduced income, potential reduction in retirement benefits (depending on how program is set up), inflation, social security earnings test ceiling, and feared loss of status when working reduced schedules. Employers have not always directly addressed these issues in providing innovative work options. Additionally, workers may be unaware of the arrangements because of low program profiles.

To illustrate, few Wisconsin state employees aged 55 and older were willing to participate in the state's pilot job sharing Project JOIN, despite special efforts to recruit participants. Project staff discovered that many employees had no idea how such a break from traditional work patterns would affect their benefits and, out of fear they would be reduced, declined involvement in the program. As the problems and questions surfaced, Wisconsin began researching the specific choices of older state employees.

Then, in 1979, the State of Wisconsin along with the University of Wisconsin began a two-and-a-half year research and demonstration project to test the viability of alternative work patterns for state employees 55 years and older. The project, conducted under a grant from the Employment and Training Administration, U.S. Department of Labor, is titled "Pre-Retirement Work Options."

Specific areas under investigation are productivity, job satisfaction, job characteristics, impact on employers, and effect on employees 55 years and older who desire to reduce their work hours. Through a grant from the Intergovernmental Personnel Act, definitive answers to retirement benefit questions were put into booklet form. This publication is now being used in the Pre-Retirement Work Options program as an informational tool for state employees interested in reducing their work hours.

Organizations also have understandably viewed early retirement, rather than extended worklives, as the trend. Factors such as relative worker affluence, collective bargaining agreements, and changing values enabled and encouraged many to retire early. However, additional factors—changing worker attitudes, inflation, demographics, the financial stability of the social security system and private pension plans—suggest that this trend may not continue.

The 1979 Harris poll showing an expressed interest by older persons in reduced work schedules also indicated that inflation is the number one problem for retirees, and a 1978 Conference Board study indicated a similar concern among retired executives. The population of older Americans—growing as a result of lengthened life expectancy and declining birth rates—may be able to translate its preferences for more flexible work and retirement patterns into policies and programs.

VOLUNTARY TIME-INCOME TRADE-OFF

County of Santa Clara

Santa Clara County, located at the south end of the San Francisco Bay, is often referred to as "Silicon Valley" because of its concentration of high technology electronic companies. The area also enjoys a relatively low unemployment rate in comparison to the rest of the United States. Santa Clara County is one of the largest counties in California with a population of 1,300,000 and employs more than 9,500 people. Approximately 65 percent of the County workforce is female, and 29 percent are minorities. Under the Myers, Milias, Brown Act of 1968—California's law governing public sector bargaining—the scope of bargaining allows all employees collective bargaining rights and includes broad interpretation for negotiating wages, hours, and working conditions. With the exception of 125 employees in the Executive Management Group, all County employees are represented by one of 21 collective bargaining units affiliated with 14 local unions. Local 715 of the Service Employees International Union (SEIU) represents the majority of employees—6,500.

Early Alternative Work Programs
Used by the County

Before implementing the Voluntary Reduced Work Hours Program (VRWH) affecting all County employees in 1976, Santa Clara County already had implemented a number of innovative work schedules to meet the needs of management and employees. Among the arrangements were split codes (half-time jobs) for which County employees could apply; staggered work hour programs where employees worked eight hours but had varying starting times; a 4-day/40-hour workweek program for sections of the Sheriff's Department; a flexitime program for sections of the County's Probation Departments; and a Time Off in-Lieu-of Income program in the early 1970s for Public Health Nurses.

These programs were negotiated in what both labor and management representatives characterize as a cooperative collective bargaining climate. Phil Giarrizzo, Supervising Field Representative of Local 715, SEIU, enumerates labor's reasons for Santa Clara's interest in developing reduced work hour strategies. First, Service Employees Locals have autonomy and can represent the needs of the memberhship based on particular circumstances in the jurisdiction, a situation that promotes a climate favorable to exploration of new programs. Second, public sector unions have been particularly subject to intense membership and public pressures because of unstable economic conditions. It was evident to SEIU many years before passage of California's Proposition 13 in 1978 that a tax revolt was brewing. Union leaders and county managers recognized the need to develop alternatives in the work scheduling for a variety of pressing reasons. The need to recognize employees' desire for leisure time and to reduce public expenditures while continuing to provide adequate service had to be recognized if the County were to retain a stable workforce.

Earlier Reduced Work Hour Programs

The 1975 collective bargaining agreement with Local 715 set aside a maximum of 400 half-time jobs. The agreement provides:

- The same hourly rate of pay for part-time workers as fulltime workers in the same job classification;
- Full fringe benefits to employees working half-time or more, except for vacation and sick leave, which are prorated based upon the number of hours worked;
- Conditions for management to deny requests (e.g., work is not divisible, qualified partners are not available when needed for split-shift positions);
- Grievance procedures for employees denied requests for part-time.

By 1979, the County employed 95 people on a part-time basis and 582 in split code positions. Most employees in split code positions are in the clerical field. (In reality, many of the split code arrangements are solo part-time positions.) The establishment of part-time positions with benefits has helped in the recruitment and retention of employees who have skills which are in demand but short supply—clerical workers, for example. However, while part-time employees provide services to the County, there are also extra costs. Pursuant to the union agreement, the County pays full health, dental, and life insurance benefits, as well as social security and Public Employees Retirement System, for employees working half-time or more. Estimates range between $.26 and $.40 on each wage dollar per employee for fringe benefits. Split codes add an additional cost for benefits for the second employee.

Even before split codes were put into effect, special reduced work hour arrangements were developed for nurses. In 1972, the County and SEIU Local 715 negotiated the Time-Off Equivalent (TOE) plan which allowed Public Health nurses to trade a 5 percent wage increase for 13 additional days off during the year (the equivalent in cost to 5 percent in salary). Executive Secretary of Local 715 Michael Baratz said that at least half of the 70 County Public Health nurses took advantage of the option. Another reduced work hour program option was negotiated for nurses in 1974. Under it, Public Health nurses were allowed to receive an additional six-and-a-half vacation days per year in exchange for a 2.5 percent pay reduction.

Development of Voluntary
Reduced Work Hour Program

Santa Clara County's experience with reduced work hour arrangements before Spring 1976 set the stage for serious consideration of a larger program when the County faced a possible $13 million deficit in the fiscal year beginning July 1, 1976.

The Santa Clara Board of Supervisors wanted to avoid layoffs but, at the same time, realized it was necessary to take concerted action to reduce the deficit for the fiscal year. It decided to reduce employment hours and salaries through an across-the-board reduction in the biweekly schedule from 80 to 75 hours. Although the unions also wanted to avoid layoffs, they strenuously objected to the unilateral action by the County management and disagreed as to what type of work sharing approach would be best. One concern was that a blanket approach would cause severe hardship for some employees.

In a series of negotiating sessions, management and labor worked to devise alternative approaches. Because of the gravity of the problem, two board members (Dan McCorquodale and Sig Sanchez) became directly involved in negotiations. SEIU's

Baratz, who had proposed a voluntary time in-lieu-of income trade-off program during the 1975 round of negotiations, was joined by representatives from the Social Services Union, Local 535, SEIU, in the negotiations.

Agreement was reached to offer a Voluntary Reduced Work Hour Program (VRWH) for all County employees as a first step in avoiding layoffs and achieving cost savings. A critical negotiating point for the unions was that the program be voluntary in nature. Also, full fringe benefit coverage was to be continued in order to secure union membership support and as an incentive for participation.

Management viewed the VRWH Program as a starting point for addressing the deficit problem but doubted there would be sufficient participation to offset the anticipated deficit. Consequently, management retained the right to take further action if the program did not succeed. The program was already underway when it became clear that the expected deficit would not materialize. At the urging of employees who wanted the option to trade work for leisure to be permanently available, the union negotiated the program into the collective bargaining agreement. Management had concluded that VRWH could save money while requiring only a slight curtailment in the large number of service programs provided by the County to the public.

The Voluntary Reduced Work Hour Program

Santa Clara County offers employees with six months prior full-time active service a 2.5 percent, 5 percent, 10 percent or 20 percent reduction in worktime and pay for a six-month period. Departmental approval is required before employees can participate and scheduling must be "mutually acceptable" to supervisors and employees. Supervisors may deny requests if participation results in overtime for other employees. Employees can renew their VRWH schedules in succeeding periods or return to full-time status at the conclusion of the contract. Reduced worktime can be taken as a few hours per day, a few days per week, or in a larger block of time, depending upon agreement between the employee and the supervisor. When all these conditions are met, both parties sign a contract which binds the employee to participate for the full six-month period.

It was expected that the reduced labor input would result in lower levels of service. Specifically written into the contract was language prohibiting work speed-ups, i.e., the County cannot require voluntary reduced work hour participants and full-time workers to work faster. During the first year of the program, service did decrease. Subsequently, as economic conditions improved for the County in the mid-1970s, the VRWH plan became an integral part of the regular employment policy. Some departments used temporary help or created additional positions to regain the former service level; in particular, this was noted in areas requiring 24-hour, 7-day continuous coverage such as Health and Hospital institutions and Juvenile and Adult Correctional facilities.

The program fringe benefit policy includes:

- Sick leave, vacation, holidays, and seniority (for layoff and pay raise purposes) which are accrued as if participants were full-time employees.
- Medical, dental, and life insurance which continue with the County paying its portion of the premium as if the employees were full-time workers.
- Prorated County retirement and social security contributions. Since retirement plan contributions depend on earnings, these fringe benefits are automatically prorated, resulting in reduced retirement benefits in certain circumstances. For example, participation in the program by employees immediately prior to retirement would reduce County retirement benefits based on highest annual earnings; therefore, these employees were advised against enrolling in the VRWH.

Participation

The number of employees participating in VRWH has varied considerably since the program started, with more than 1,500 workers (or 17 percent of the County workforce) involved in 1976 and fewer than 450 (4.5 percent of the workforce) in 1979. Interest has fluctuated with changes in the economy (workers are less willing to reduce their hours during periods of high inflation), with time of year (there is a general preference for reduced hours in spring and summer), and fear of a layoff.

When VRWH was first implemented in 1976, about 1,600 employees applied and more than 1,500 were approved. While Social Services departments in many other California counties had to lay off employees during 1976 and 1977, Santa Clara County was able to avoid layoffs, in part because of the large participation in Voluntary Reduced Work Hours by employees of the department.

Statistics show that the first time this program was offered, close to 71 percent of the participants were female. A breakdown of the participants' selections in 1976 follows:

- 55 percent selected the 5 percent reduction, which aggregates to 52 additional hours off work during the six-month period;
- 26 percent selected the 10 percent reduction, or 104 additional hours off work;
- 17 percent selected the 20 percent reduction, or 208 additional hours off work.

Most participants were clerical workers, health professionals, and social workers—many for the Department of Social Services, who were particularly concerned about being affected by a layoff.

In the second year of the program the number of requests decreased to 700, with 675 approved. The sharp decrease in participation is believed to be a direct result of reduced fear of immediate layoff. However, other factors such as personal need, outside interests, season of the year, and personal finances all have been mentioned by individuals as reasons for losing interest in continuing participation in the program. Among the disincentives to participation noted by unions were inflation and a negative environment created by management which discouraged workers from requesting participation.

For the six-month period October 1979 through March 1980, 440 requests were granted.

- 5 percent of employees took the 2.5 percent option;
- 29 percent took the 5 percent option;
- 40 percent took the 10 percent option;
- 26 percent took the 20 percent option.

Exhibit A shows a breakdown by occupation for County employees participating in this program.

Participation Considerations

Two issues concerning participation by specific groups have arisen during the course of this program. One was resolved by permitting participation, the other by forbidding it. The County Executive ruled in the first instance that County employees whose County employment was funded through the Comprehensive Employment and Training Act (CETA) or received food stamps were eligible to participate. Questions had been raised as to the appropriateness of allowing CETA workers to participate in a "vacation program."

The other case involved employees in the Municipal Court System who, though paid by the County and covered by the County's collective bargaining agreements, have their employment hours and working conditions determined by the California Courts System. The state legislature grants judges authority over the "conduct" and "personal privileges" provided these employees. The Court took the position that its workload requirements were too heavy to permit participation in voluntary reduced work hour programs. According to union representatives, there has been some worker resentment.

Program Costs

The money saved by departments through the VRWH Program was credited to the applicable departments until the start of fiscal year 1980-81 when the Board of Supervisors began reallocating the savings to human service programs.

The County maintains raw cost data for each VRWH Program. This information is periodically used to track trends on cost as well as usage. The County's gross estimated savings in the six-month program which ended March 1980 totalled $420,000. However, no adjustment was made for administrative costs to the program, higher fringe benefit cost per labor hour of participants, overtime for some employees, and the additional cost of hiring temporary employees to cover staff shortages for employees participating in the program.

Exhibit A

Breakdown of Participants in Voluntary Reduced Work Hour Program Between October 1979 and April 1980

Department	2.5 percent	5 percent	10 percent	20 percent	Total
Assessor - PAA	3	18	5		26
County Counsel	1	1	1		3
CETA			2	4	6
Registrar/Records - PAA	1			1	2
Data Processing - PAA			8		8
County Exec. - OMB				1	1
Communications - EMA/GSA		5			5
Family Support - DA	1				1
District Attorney		1			1
Career Criminal - DA		1			1
Pre-Trial Release		1			1
Adult Prob-Drinking Driver			1		1
Adult Probation		1	5	5	11
Juvenile Probation	1	10	3	1	15
Public Services - EMA/GSA	2	3	5	1	11
EMA/GSA		3	3	2	8
Health Services	4	34	32	31	101
Public Health - Mental	4	13	18	16	51
Public Health - Methadone			1	1	2
Substance Abuse - MH		1			1
Public Health - Alcoholism			3	3	6
Social Services - Admin	3	23	75	38	139
Soc. Ser - Manpower Prog	1				1
Transportation Development	1		1		2
Transportation Aviation			1		1
County Library	1	10	13	10	34
Parks - EMA/GSA			1	2	3
VMC		1	1		2
TOTALS	23	126	179	116	444

All in all, neither the aggregate savings to the County nor the reduction of service was as great as initially anticipated.

Managerial Considerations

Managers and department heads initially reluctant to reduce their staff hours were encouraged by the Board of Supervisors and the County Executive to grant as many requests as possible. These managers were concerned that the board would interpret the lower number of total work hours as an indication that some staff were not really needed and ultimately would reduce the departments' budget allocation. Denial of request is not officially a grievable offense, but during the first year the Board of Supervisors asked department heads who had turned down several requests to justify their positions at a public board meeting. (Denials now are handled informally by union and management representatives.) The action by the Board of Supervisors put pressure on department heads to consider requests seriously and to try to make the program work.

When economic conditions improved, managers already were experienced in the program implementation and were less reluctant to grant employee requests. Some of their initial fears were realized however, as some department budgets were cut and reallocated—though not necessarily because of the VRWH Program.

VRWH has created more administrative work for County personnel, department heads, and supervisors in requiring careful scheduling and shifting of personnel between part- and full-time schedules. As a result, managers have gained a very clear understanding of staffing levels and workload needs in their departments.

In addition to the voluntary reduced work hour program, the County offers various flexitime and compressed week schedules. While each nontraditional work option has its unique advantages, management notes the co-mingling of a number of flexible work hour options within the same program or department can cause considerable difficulties for management and can require a substantial amount of time and effort to coordinate staffing and work activities among the various programs. Ideally, these approaches should be complementary. However, sometimes the schedules do not mesh well and require adjustments to ensure satisfactory service to the public as well as internal coordination.

Reasons for Program Success

Overall the program has been viewed as successful; the County has saved money, the program seems to be meeting the needs of the employees and management, and some of the County operations have improved.

Labor and management representatives agree that top management support was an essential factor in ensuring the viability of VRWH. They feel that bringing the union into the decisionmaking process early led to an airing of concerns and a subsequent satisfactory resolution. One reason for the high degree of participation by County employees was the continuation of fringe benefits. Another is that Santa Clara County employees receive somewhat higher salaries than those of other counties to stay competitive with nearby high technology firms, thereby enabling more workers to consider foregoing some income for leisure time.

Conclusion

The nature and scope of the voluntary reduced work hour program has changed over time to respond to different economic conditions and employee preferences. What was initially a crisis response evolved into a permanent program. As Baratz notes, "the attractiveness of the 6-month reduced work hour contract is the flexibility it provides and its acknowledgement that some employees want transient time-off. Participating employees are not saying that they want to work part-time for the rest of their careers, but rather that they want reduced hours time for a particular half-year period to pursue other endeavors."

Through VRWH, the County saved money and avoided layoffs. It also generated considerable goodwill among its employees. In the long run, it gained flexibility in allocating its human and financial resources. The plan, in fact, was so well received that neighboring San Mateo County, whose employees are represented by Local 715, SEIU, and Local 829, American Federation of State, County, and Municipal Employees, developed a similar arrangement.

VOLUNTARY TIME-INCOME TRADE-OFF

New York State Department of Taxation and Finance and the Civil Service Employees Association, AFSCME, AFL-CIO

The New York State Department of Taxation and Finance is a large state agency with a workforce of 6,000. The department has a centralized operation for processing all of New York State's seven million tax returns. This centralized system requires two huge data processing centers, one of the world's largest mailrooms, and a file system for storing the returns.

Decisionmaking

A combination of factors—a desire to increase morale among entry-level employees in the Taxation and Finance Department, a wish to create more summer jobs for college students, and a need to reduce costs without reducing operating efficiency—led to the adoption in Summer 1980 of a voluntary time-income trade-off program for selected workers. Referred to as TOTS, or Take Off The Summer, the project was designed primarily to give working mothers an opportunity to remain at home during their children's school vacation. For some of the mothers in the program, summer child care costs approached the level of their net income from the state job. Since the positions involved were entry-level, the replacement of permanent personnel wasn't expected to cause production problems. Additionally, it was hoped that the project's leave without pay feature might enable the department to reduce costs without affecting operational efficiency.

A labor relations staff member, Thomas J. Donnelly, suggested the TOTS approach, which builds on a practice operating in the private sector. The Director of Agency Manpower Management, Daniel F. Halloran, liked the idea and discussed it with the department's Civil Service Employee Association (CSEA) representative, who also reacted positively.

The program was then presented to the Deputy Commissioner for Program and Policy, Frederick G. Hicks, who approved implementation. The Deputy Commissioner was particularly pleased about meeting an objective of employing a larger number of students during the summer months; in previous summers requests had exceeded available summer job openings.

Program

The TOTS Project allowed entry-level Tax and Finance Department employees to take leaves of absence without pay for 8 to 12 weeks during the summer of 1980. Leave had to be taken for a minimum of 8 of the 12 weeks between June 19 and September 11, and in one block of time.

Participation during the 1980 trial was restricted to eligible employees (i.e., those who had completed probation by February 1, 1980) in six job titles in entry-level Grade III (GS 1-5 positions): clerk, file clerk, typist, data entry machine operator, mail and supply clerk, and mail and supply helper. Approximately 850 employees (60 percent of whom were women) were eligible.

Employees were advised of the program through the December 1979 issue of the New York State Department of Taxation and Finance newspaper, "Tax Topics." A lead article described the program and included an application form. The program was also described in other internal publications.

Most fringe benefits remained in force during the leave time. Participants did have to pay health insurance premiums (the department issued a coupons book with due dates) and CSEA dues directly.

The leave did not count toward retirement or in computation of such things as preference for overtime and vacation scheduling. On the other hand, the lost time did not affect the seniority date for layoff purposes.

More than 100 employees applied for the program, and 55 became participants, most of them mothers whose annual earnings averaged $8,000-$9,000.

Evaluation

At the direction of State Taxation and Finance Commissioner James H. Tully, formal evaluation of the project was conducted to determine whether the program should be expanded. Manpower Director Halloran said the following issues were considered:

- Were there cost reductions?
- Did nonparticipating employees resent those who took advantage of the unpaid leave policy?
- Were there disruptions in the operation of the Department?
- Did the workers on leave return to the job rejuvenated, or did they resent returning to work?

Findings showed a substantial cost savings to the Department. Savings in salaries for participating employees amounted to $73,123.97 plus another $22,127.31 in savings for fringe benefits. College students were hired to replace TOTS employees at a cost of $48,311.36, approximately $15,000 less than originally budgeted for replacements. Hourly workers may have social security and retirement contributions deducted but the summer replacements decided against the deductions. Further, hourly workers employed less than six months are not eligible to receive medical coverage or accrue leave time.

Agency Labor Relations Representative Thomas J. Donnelly of the Labor Relations Bureau that prepared the evaluation report notes that, in addition to salaries and fringe benefits, the cost of training and hiring replacements was considered. Hiring costs were negligible as interviews were conducted in one large pool and placements were then immediately assigned to specific jobs. The Bureau also distributed questionnaires to employees and supervisors to determine how much time was spent in training temporary hourly workers and retraining annual salaried employees upon their return. Actual replacement training amounted to less than one day. One hundred percent of returning annual employees felt they needed no retraining other than familiarization with any new procedures implemented during their absence.

Although all but one participant said they would have been able to continue working through the summer without TOTS, they observed they would have encountered childcare difficulties. Donnelly says that in a time of two wage earners or single parent families, TOTS provides employees with "a valuable tool to strengthen their family structure."

According to the president of the local chapter of CSEA, Carmen Bagnoli, employee response was overwhelmingly positive. Some supervisory personnel applied for the program, and Bagnoli notes that one applicant—ineligible for the program because of her higher grade level—said she would take a permanent demotion so she could participate.

The Department concluded that TOTS improved the morale of participants who returned to work in September with a better perspective about themselves, their families, and their jobs. Supervisors generally agreed that productivity was reasonably maintained by the replacements. Significantly, 92 percent of supervisors involved in TOTS felt the Department should continue the program.

Commissioner Tully notes that the positive reaction of both supervisors and employees is the "highest accolade an innovative program like this can receive." In sum, Department officials regard the TOTS program as an innovative idea that allows the Department to save money, improve employee morale, and provide sorely needed jobs to students.

Due to the Department's highly successul experience with TOTS in 1980, Commissioner Tully has expanded the 1981 program to extend eligibility to many more employees. This year, applications were accepted from eligible employees in the Administrative or Operational Services Unit in positions up to and including Grand 17 and employees in positions designated PS&T or M/C up to and including Grade 22.

VOLUNTARY TIME-INCOME TRADE-OFF

Alameda County Public Defenders Department

The Alameda County Public Defenders Department, California, employs 101 attorneys to serve nine court locations in the county. Most attorneys are members of the Alameda County Public Defenders Association (ACPDA).

Decisionmaking

Because of the intense pressures involved—the public defenders have burdensome case loads and frequently work 60-to 80-hour weeks—burnout has been a problem, according to Chief of the Defenders Office James Jenner. For several months during 1975, Jenner and former Chief James Hooley developed a strategy with members of ACPDA to alleviate stress by providing time away from the job during which attorneys could refresh themselves. Together they developed the voluntary time-income trade-off option.

In addition to reducing the problem of employee burnout, the program was expected to help in the following areas:

* Improve the quality of client representation;
* Reduce turnover, especially of experienced, well-qualified employees;
* Serve as a recruitment incentive to attract bright law students;
* Save the county money, at least in the short run, by replacing experienced attorneys on leave with young attorneys paid entry-level salaries.

Program

Attorneys have the option of working 10 or 11 months at their regular monthly salaries and taking up to 2 months unpaid leave. The Public Defender meets with ACPDA each year to determine the aggregate number of months available for unpaid leave, based on office budget and staffing considerations. The length of the leave period (i.e., six 2-month or twelve 1-month intervals) also is determined at these meetings. In 1979, for example, the agreement was for a total of 48 months leave time, to be taken in 2-month intervals.

The aggregate amount and length of leave may vary from year to year, but once an agreement is reached, adherence is strict. Since the courts operate throughout the year and the office must have adequate staffing each month, ACPDA is required to provide the precise number of attorneys for each period. Efforts are made first to distribute leave months by employee choice. Once months are filled this way, the remaining months are distributed by lot (i.e., chance drawing). If an attorney changes his/her mind after agreeing to a particular schedule, the individual must find a replacement or not get paid. This strict requirement is needed, says Jenner, for the program to work efficiently.

Attorneys may combine leave with regular paid vacations, providing a substantial period of time away from work to pursue educational and leisure activities.

During the unpaid leave, employees are individually responsible for covering all fringe benefit costs, including medical insurance.

Participation

All attorneys who have completed the basic 2.5-year training program are eligible to participate in the voluntary time-income trade-off plan. Since 1975, approximately two-thirds of the attorneys have taken unpaid leave at one time or another. Bob Foster, Assistant Public Defender and former president of ACPDA, estimates that 60 employees have been consistent users of the plan. He observes that a majority of these attorneys are single—those who not only receive a tax break by working a shorter workyear but who wish to and are financially able to spend more time on other interests. Another 20 attorneys have used the time-income trade-off option periodically for such specific purposes as special vacations or extended maternity leaves.

Nonprofessional staff are ineligible for participation but have not requested a similar arrangement; this is probably a matter of economics.

Impact

Because of the built-in flexibility of the plan, the program has enabled the county and employees to meet different goals.

- Job Creation. In the first year of the program, the county increased the number of attorneys without increasing its budget. County hiring practices pemitted Hooley to employ new full-time "substitute" attorneys in direct proportion to the number of employees agreed upon for leaves. For example, four new attorneys were hired in 1975. These entry-level attorneys received lower compensation than more experienced defenders. The differential amounted to about $800 per month per employee, constituting a saving of $30,000 to $40,000 that year.

- Job Preservation. Following the passage of Proposition 13, the county budget for fiscal 1978-79 was cut. The Public Defenders Department anticipated a loss of 14 or 15 attorneys. The Public Defender and the Association expanded the total number of leave months. Once they explained the situation to all attorneys, a sufficient number signed up for the program so that several lay-offs were avoided. Additional attorneys were laid off, but all of them eventually returned to work as the result of the expanded program and normal attrition.

- Morale. According to county administrators and employees, the program has achieved its original goal. Morale has improved and attorneys are returning from their leave time with their "batteries recharged."

- Retention. Jenner notes that the voluntary time-income trade-off provides some of the Department's most experienced and skilled attorneys (generally those with the most complex cases) experiencing the symptom of burnout an incentive to remain. While turnover in the Department decreased by 9 percent in the year following the program's implementation, management attributes the decline to a number of factors. One was a changing, more positive attitude by the legal profession toward public defense work. In addition to the impact of the trade-off program, there has been a gradual decline in the number of jobs for attorneys, and county employees may be less inclined to leave their jobs when other positions are unavailable in the area.

Conclusion

The option provides attorneys in the Alameda County Public Defenders Office an opportunity to temporarily or permanently (within the constraints of the agreement) shorten their workyear. In a profession in which part-time work is associated with severe career repercussions, the option, says Jenner, has provided a successful reduced work hour strategy in meeting the changing needs of the county and its attorneys. In fact, the Public Defender's Office expanded the program in 1980 to its Investigation Department, which employs 26 people. Jenner points out that "while there are definite benefits from the standpoint of improved morale and retention, the program is not without administrative and technical difficulties."

SABBATICALS

McDonald's Corporation

Ray Kroc, founder of McDonald's Corporation, opened his first fast food restaurant on April 15, 1955, in suburban Illinois. Today, 25 years later, the McDonald's chain dominates the fast food industry, with more than 6,000 restaurants throughout the United States and in 23 countries. Approximately 70 percent of McDonald's restaurants are franchised; the company owns the remaining outlets, approximately 1,500 restaurants employing more than 100,000 workers. Employees are nonunionized. Most work part time in direct restaurant service; only 13,000 work full time. Headquartered in Oak Brook, Illinois, McDonald's has 25 regional offices.

Organizational Climate

McDonald's continued growth and sustained performance is attributed largely to the drive, determination, and enthusiasm of founder Kroc. His entrepreneurial, hands-on management style is indelibly stamped on McDonald's philosophy and operating policies. As the company's 20th anniversary publication points out, "The McDonald's story has been more than a story of a business. It has been the story of people."

From the beginning Kroc sought people wanting a challenge and willing to work long hours for financial reward. "The old timers," the publication recalls, "were in the business heart and soul, 7 days a week. They were eating, sleeping McDonald's and that's why they made a success and made McDonald's a success."

McDonald's current recruiting brochure continues to emphasize individual performance as the critical factor in sustaining the company's phenomenal growth. The company's belief in the importance of the individual in the McDonald's system is reflected in its creation in 1976 of an Office of Vice President, Individuality. At the same time, McDonald's fosters an esprit de corps and strong company identification among employees through awards, anniversary celebrations, and medals. Another aspect of the company's philosophy is commitment to the welfare of the community.

Program Development

A few years ago management grew concerned that its work ethic of strong company commitment, hard work, and long hours, sustained over many years, could lead to employee burnout. Jim Kuhn, Vice President, Individuality, was assigned in 1977 to investigate innovative approaches to the problem. After looking at university sabbaticals and the extended vacation options in the steel and aluminum industries, Kuhn designed McDonald's Bonus Vacation Program.

The program's purpose is "to recognize the importance of each individual's life outside of McDonald's, to allow people the time to pursue their dreams and return to work with a fresh outlook, to reward extra effort and long hours put in by our people." At the time of adoption, the company had a number of employees in their mid-thirties who had begun their careers with McDonald's as teenagers and thus had spent 15 to 20 years in the stressful environment.

Program

All full-time employees are eligible for a fully paid bonus vacation of eight weeks for every 10 years of company service. (Eligibility for former part-time employees who later converted to full-time is based on the start of full-time employment.) The company encourages employees to combine bonus vacation with regular vacation leave, resulting in a total of 11 weeks of vacation at the end of 10 years of service and 13 weeks at the end of 20 years of service. Employees may take the bonus vacation any time during their anniversary year or within five calendar years. For example, employees with 10 years of service must take the eight weeks sometime before the end of their 15th year of service.

To ensure that the bonus vacation meets the company objective of allowing people to return to work with a fresh outlook, management placed some restrictions on leave usage:

- Leave cannot be exchanged for a lump sum payment and is forfeited should an employee terminate employment.

- All bonus leave must be taken at the same time (leave cannot, for example, be split into single week increments), preferably in conjunction with vacation leave.

Participation

Although the company encourages all eligible employees to use the bonus vacation, it has not mandated participation. Kuhn believes that forcing employees to take the leave would be paternalistic and inconsistent with McDonald's philosophy.

Management does not keep track of employee eligibility. Eligible employees must notify supervisors of their intent to use the leave and work out coverage at the office level.

While participation in the plan has been small—21 participants in 1978 and 30 in 1979—employees at all occupational levels (including secretaries, store managers, technicians, and officers) have taken advantage of it.

Management suggests several possible explanations for the limited usage. First, the company is young and has experienced rapid growth, and many of its employees are not yet eligible for the bonus leave. Second, the deadline for participation for those eligible for the leave when the program started has not passed; other employees may take advantage of the program before their 1982 deadline. Third, many eligible workers initially were reluctant to leave work for eight or more weeks.

Impact on Employer

Because of favorable informal responses, McDonald's has not made any efforts to evaluate the bonus vacation rigorously, says the company's Manager of Benefits and Compensation, Doug Clark. "We don't see any need to monitor it more closely," he explained. "Comments from employees indicate that the company's objectives are being met. Employees return rested, with a new perspective on their work."

Although there are short term costs, management believes that these will be offset in the long run by retention of high-performance workers whose creativity has been revitalized.

An outcome of the program has been an enhanced perception of McDonald's as employer by current and prospective corporate employees. Employees remark that benefits such as the bonus vacation plan show that McDonald's cares for its employees. The reaction of a secretary to the program underscores this attitude: "What is unique about McDonald's is its knack for designing benefits rewarding all people, at all levels of the company. The company lets you know that your efforts are appreciated while you're still here."

Effect on Employees

While a majority of participants are enthusiastic about the bonus leave once they've taken advantage of it, most experience anxieties initially. Almost all participants who were informally interviewed said they had been apprehensive about being absent from work for an extended period of time, given the character of McDonald's work environment. They worried that if their office could get along without them for three months, their supervisors might decide they were not really needed.

Participants agree that the bonus vacation provides a much needed respite from work. For many, it was the first time they had had substantial leisure time to pursue their chosen activities without financial worry. Some took long-dreamed-of trips. Others remained at home gardening, remodelling, or spending time with their families. Project Engineer Joseph Moser says the most rewarding aspect of his bonus vacation was taking daily bike rides with his teenage daughter and chatting with her about her concerns.

Participants noted they had numerous adjustment problems. After years of getting up early each morning to rush to work, some found their biological clocks did not adjust rapidly to the new, more flexible lifestyle. During the first few weeks of leave, they thought of the office frequently. Later these anxieties disappeared, and they began to relax and enjoy themselves. Feelings of isolation cropped up for some. One man finished his project of building an additional bedroom to his home earlier than anticipated. Without the companionship of his spouse, friends, and children, who were at work and school, he soon began to feel alone and isolated, out of touch with the rest of the world. To overcome these feelings, he undertook further remodelling projects and jokingly remarked, "I was glad the leave finally came to an end—before I went bankrupt!"

Participating employees stress the need for adequate preparation if the person is to enjoy his or her leisure time. A few people who thought they would have no problems keeping busy found the abundance of free time so distressing that they returned to work, forfeiting the remainder of their leave.

Employees anticipated difficulty reentering work after such a long absence. However, for most employees this problem did not materialize. Ron Hebert, a project engineer, summed up the feelings of many employees. "After a few days back, it was as if I had never left."

McDonald's management believes these fears inhibit many eligible employees from using their bonus vacation. Although the company does not provide any formal counseling, supervisors do encourage potential participants to discuss their concerns about the leave with those who have returned. Since the vast majority of employees who have taken the leave are overwhelmingly enthusiastic about the benefits of the bonus vacation, many supervisors have noticed that these discussions dispel employees' anxieties and more employees begin to seriously consider using their leave.

SABBATICALS

ROLM Corporation

The ROLM Corporation of Santa Clara, California, is a non-unionized manufacturer of military and industrial computers and the CBX computerized business telephone systems. A fast-growing company in a high technology industry where rapid growth is normal, ROLM has experienced an annual growth of 50 to 100 percent since it was founded in 1969. Annual sales have increased to more than $100 million, and the number of employees has increased to more than 2,000 (from 107 in 1973).

Founders Gene Richardson, M. Kenneth Oshman, Walter Loewenstern, Jr., and Robert Maxfield attribute the company's success to their "individual but complementary" efforts as financier, businessman, engineer, and marketer. Central to their management style is their belief in the talents of individuals, reflected in the various company reports and recruiting publications:

All achievement begins with the efforts of the individual.
The ROLM idea. . . is a philosophy that encourages individual ideas, individual effort, individual achievement.
Behind our success are the efforts of exceptional people.

To attract and retain skilled and talented workers in a competitive market, ROLM offers a benefits package that it terms "one of the most generous in this or any other industry." Benefits range from more traditional ones—medical and dental insurance for all full-time and part-time employees who work more than 30 hours a week, life, disability, vacation, sick and holiday pay, and a profit sharing plan—to benefits that Vice President Loewenstern terms "extraordinary," including an onsite recreation center and a 3-month paid sabbatical for workers who have completed certain service requirements.

Program Development

Loewenstern observes that the type of people the company recruits—highly qualified and achievement oriented—are subject to great stress in the fast paced rapidly changing field of high technology. Management grew concerned about the problem of employee burnout and thought some time off might reduce the incidence of burnout. Adapting a traditional model, the university sabbatical program, to the corporation, President Oshman designed a sabbatical program for employees to provide time for rejuvenation and broadening of personal experiences. Termed Continuous Service Leave (CSL), the program began in 1974.

Continuous Service Leave

After six years of continuous, full-time service and every seven years thereafter, all ROLM employees, from unskilled to president, are eligible for 12 weeks of leave with full pay and continued benefits. Employees can combine the leave with regular vacation time.

Since the program's intent is to provide employees some relief from work pressures for an extended period, ROLM places few restrictions on how the leave is used. However, there are certain requirements:

- Leave must be taken all at once; unused leave is forfeited.
- Employees cannot trade leave for its cash equivalent.
- Any compensation the employee receives from another source during leave time is deducted from salary.
- Employees must notify their supervisors in advance when they intend to use the leave.

Participation

Because ROLM is a young company in an industry of highly mobile workers, only a small number of employees have been eligible for the leave, although that number is increasing steadily. In January 1980, 60 employees were eligible for continuous service leave, up from 30 the year before.

All eligible employees have taken advantage of continuous service leave. Some, like Loewenstern, have taken long-planned trips abroad. One employee built a dream house. Still others spent the time reevaluating their career plans and rethinking their values.

Impact on Employer

The company estimates the cost of CSL at .4 to .6 percent of ROLM's payroll. The company believes this is a small price to pay for a benefit as attractive as CSL. According to Loewenstern, the employes talk about it a lot.

There has been some employee turnover as a result of the program: 10 to 20 percent of employees who took the leave left ROLM a few months after they returned to work. "The cost for those individuals who have chosen to leave," notes Loewenstern, "is a small price for six years of efficient and productive work. At any rate, if an employee returns dissatisfied, it probably is better for both the company and the employee that the employee leaves." Most employees come back refreshed and ready to accept new challenges.

Loewenstern cites several beneficial side effects of the program:

- Facilitates cross training. Since workers are gone for 3 months, remaining employees may learn new skills or experiment with different jobs.
- Destroys the myth of indispensibility. In a results-oriented work environment such as ROLM's, some employees become so involved in their work that neither they nor their supervisors believe the company could survive without them. Continuous service leave puts this idea into perspective.
- Encourages employees to catch up on backlog. Busy employees who have fallen behind in some project have a reason to bring all their projects up-to-date before they leave.

In sum, employees like the program and the company has realized some benefits from it. Management has taken a hard-nosed look at its impact, however.

Located in California's "Silicon Valley," ROLM recruits in a highly competitive market. Management believes that continuous service leave, in itself, has no substantial impact on employee recruitment and retention. It is, according to Loewenstern, a combination of challenging work, pay, fringe benefits, and a good work environment (attractive buildings, recreation center, flexible hours, etc.) that attracts and retains workers.

SABBATICALS

Wells Fargo & Company

Wells Fargo, a nonunionized international banking corporation, is the third largest bank in California, eleventh largest in the country. Headquartered in San Francisco, Wells Fargo has more than 390 branch offices throughout California. At the end of 1979, the company employed more than 18,000 persons on a full-time equivalency basis. Minorities comprise 35 percent of personnel and women 70 percent; of company officers, managers, and professionals, more than 21 percent are minority and 52 percent female.

In 1977, Wells Fargo designed a Personal Growth Leave program as a reward for long-time employees. Employees with 15 years of service (about 9 percent of Wells Fargo employees) are eligible to take up to three months of fully paid leave to pursue personal interests not necessarily related to their jobs. While there are few restrictions, the company's intent is that the activities be "serious and intense as compared to. . . diversionary and escapist."

Each year, an aggregate of 12 months leave is available. Only one employee may be on Personal Growth Leave at any one time. Participants are guaranteed either the same job or a job at the same grade, salary, and comparable responsibility upon return.

Employees interested in a Personal Growth Leave must submit a written application describing the activity they plan to pursue and indicating how the activity will broaden their perspectives. A screening committee reviews the applications and interviews applicants.

By 1980, four employees (three male and one female) had participated in the program. All were in executive-level positions.

The Personal Growth Leaves that have been approved are indicative of the wide range of activities considered acceptable. One senior trust officer took a 3-month break to study with master sculptors in Paris and Florence. A vice president spent six weeks in England, Ireland, and Scotland tracing his family tree, then did additional genealogical research in America and organized other materials which he hopes to develop into a book. Personal Growth Leave was used by an assistant vice president, a writer of prose and poetry, to produce a book of poetry. A bank officer used her leave to take several teaching courses to improve her teaching of religion to 60 inner-city children at a Saturday morning school.

Robert Leet, Senior Vice President and chairman of the Corporate Responsibility Committee, refers to the company's pride in a program that enables employees to become involved and enrich their lives. "It makes good sense for everybody—the bank, the community, and the employee."

SOCIAL SERVICE LEAVE

Xerox Corporation

Xerox was formed in 1957 as successor to the Haloid Company, a small Rochester photographic paper firm. Its development of Xerography resulting in Xeroxing becoming synonomous with copy reproduction. When the first Xerox copier was sold in 1961, the company's annual budget totaled $1 million and its workforce numbered 400 employees. By 1979, Xerox had grown nationally and internationally to a multibillion dollar firm with more than 160 affiliates employing 55,000 people in the United States alone. Approximately 15 percent of the workforce is unionized.

Even while it grew, the company maintained and expanded the principles of social concern and community participation that motivated management at Haloid. Its chief executive officer during its time of growth stated that to move forward, Xerox would have to "combine the force of technology with the force of humanism."

Xerox has termed its programs that support educational, social, and cultural activities its Social Involvement Program. The program goals are straightforward:

- To preserve and invigorate our communities;
- To help higher education prepare tomorrow's leaders;
- To stimulate volunteerism;
- To promote involvement of Xerox people;
- To give a dimension of difference to Xerox.

To expand its commitment, the company initiated in 1973 the Xerox Community Involvement Program (XCIP), which enables volunteer groups of employees to work on specific local problems with the assistance of modest company contributions to the nonprofit organization. Another approach to stimulate community involvement among employees, begun a year earlier, is the Social Service Leave (SSL) program, which permits Xerox employees to take paid time off from their jobs to participate in social projects.

Decisionmaking

Social Service Leave was the idea of Archie R. McCardell, president and chief operating officer of Xerox in 1970. Following a grant presentation that year to a major west coast university, McCardell and the company's personnel director discussed future corporate approaches on their return flight. McCardell talked about his desire to create innovative programs that would be beyond giving money. He wanted to design an approach that would share what he regarded as Xerox's most valuable resource, its employees. By the time the plane landed on the east coast, the two had sketched out the format of the Social Service Leave program.

The program officially was established in 1972. The time lag was due to the company's belief that social involvement, as good business as well as beneficial to society, must be approached as are other major business activities, with research and planning, strict budgeting and review, involving experienced professional management and having the interest and commitment of senior management.

Social Service Leave Program

Xerox allocates 264 months of employee time each year to SSL. All full-time employees with at least three years of service and in good standing with the company can apply for the leave. Both union and nonunion employees are eligible. The leave period may be as short as 1 and as long as 12 months. While on leave, employees receive full pay, retain all fringe benefits, and continue to accrue vacation time. Participating employees maintain seniority provided they return to Xerox as soon as the leave is completed. Employees are guaranteed that they can return to the same job or one similar in pay, responsibility, and opportunity for growth.

While a wide range of projects is acceptable—employees don't have to plan something "heroic, spectacular or self-sacrificing"—there are certain criteria, including:

- The project must be a program or activity sponsored by an existing nonpartisan, nonprofit organization.
- The organization must submit a written acceptance of what the employee proposes to do.

Employees initiate the request for leave. They develop projects in which they are personally interested, seek to interest the non-profit groups, and submit a written application to Xerox along with the letter of support from the community group.

Employees do not need the permission of their supervisors to apply. Nor do they need the permission of their managers to go on leave if their application is approved. If an employee's work is considered essential, the nature of the employee's work is reviewed by top management and the final decision is made by the company's president and chief operating officer.

The company does not formally evaluate participants once they undertake their leave projects, but it does ask employees to make monthly reports. At least once during the leave someone from Xerox visits each leavetaker to see how the project is progressing. Upon return to the company, employees prepared reports on their leave, outlining what was accomplished, evaluating the leave, and providing suggestions for program improvements.

Employees may reapply for another leave after three years, but only four have done so. The one employee who was granted a second leave had designed a computer system for the regional Muscular Dystrophy office that had proved so useful to the association that he adapted the system for nationwide use during his second leave.

Selection Process

Applications for SSL appear each October in the "Xerox World" magazine. Employees must submit their written applications by January 15 of each year, describing the goals of the project and the need for it. A seven-member Employee Evaluation Committee reviews all applications and allocates the 264 months total leave available.

The Committee is composed of a cross section of Xerox employees chosen for their familiarity with the program and their knowledge of community volunteer activities. Usually, it includes a leavetaker from a previous year and one just returning from leave, an employee active in community activities, and another who has participated in the selection process before.

Each year in late January, the Committee meets at a Xerox facility to consider applications. Each committee member has one vote and the Committee's decision is final. Program Manager Joseph M. Cahalan attends the meetings to facilitate the decisionmaking process but does not vote.

In the first round, each member reads all the applications in alphabetical order, rating each on a scale of 1 to 5. Members who know an applicant or are familiar with the proposed volunteer agency refrain from comment during this phase. The Committee rates the applications against several criteria, including the following:

- Applicant. Does the applicant seem committed to the project? Does he/she have the skills to do the job? Has he/she demonstrated any previous involvement in community activities through volunteer work?
- Project. Are the project objectives spelled out? Are the goals realistic? Will the project make a difference in the community?
- Sponsoring Organization. Is the sponsoring organization nonpartisan and nonprofit? Does the agency serve a useful purpose in the community?

Following this phase, the Committee discusses the applications as a group. Individual application scores may be raised or lowered as a result of comparison. Cahalan groups the high-, medium-, and low-scoring applications into separate bundles. Before low-scoring applications are eliminated from further consideration, a final review is made.

The Committee then begins the approval process, starting with the highest scoring applications. In some instances, it might recommend that the applicant devote more time than originally requested, in other instances less.

Cahalan says that the most difficult part of the review process is deciding how much leave time to approve among the middle-scoring applications, particularly since all the leave time does not have to be allocated. The Committee arrives at a consensus through further discussion and debate. "The review process," says Cahalan, "is one of the most democratic is the company."

Participation

Between 1972 and 1980, more than 300 Xerox employees participated in the Social Service Leave program. Approximately 70 employees apply for leave each year and, on an average, 28 employees are approved.

Participants represent Xerox facilities across the United States and a range of occupational levels, including sales and technical service respresentatives, secretaries, factory workers, engineers, and vice presidents; about half are in sales, repair, and clerical/administrative fields.

Despite the differences in geographic location and occupation, the profile of SSL participants has remained fairly constant. Most are married with children. The average age of the leavetaker is 36 (the youngest was 22 years, the oldest 59 years). Their median education level is 16 years, and most have an average of 6 years of service at the company. Approximately 70 percent of participants are male, 25 percent are minority, and 40 percent are nonexempt workers.

Each year, the company analyzes how the leave time has been allocated. The following chart gives the breakdown through 1979.

Project concern	Number of participants
Minority and youth counseling and training	58
Retarded and handicapped	39
Education	32
Drug and alcohol rehabilitation	17
Medical aid and legal counseling/advocacy	25
Community centers	18
Prisons	13
Miscellaneous, including art restoration, rural development in India, technical assistance	204

Reentry

Leavetakers are under no obligation to return to Xerox at the end of their leave, but all but six have done so when they completed their leave project.

More than two-thirds of the participants have returned to the same job they left. Cahalan observes that even for them, reentry requires planning and increased communication between management and returning participant. As a first step in the readjustment process, a member of the Employee Evaluation Committee visits the participant during the leave period. Cahalan contacts the employees closer to project completion and works with them in job placement and adjustment. While some employees find reentry to the workplace difficult after a long absence, most, according to Cahalan, have few problems.

Impact on the Company

Management Objectives. Management believes that Social Service Leave has successfully met company objectives of involving employees in worthwhile community activities. Cahalan attributes this success to the commitment of top management to make the program work. Over eight years, only two supervisors formally requested that an employee be prevented from taking the leave, and top management denied both requests. Cahalan notes that at Xerox, an employee's indispensibility is regarded as an indicator of poor management.

Coverage. The leavetakers' job responsibilities are handled in a variety of ways during their absence: cross-training co-workers, hiring part-time employees and consultants, and transferring other Xerox employees. These do not present major problems for the company, which is accustomed to handling job transfers as well as coverage during routine vacations and long-term absences.

Cost. Xerox spends approximately $600,000 on leavetaker salaries and $150,000 on program administration each year. Cahalan believes that, in the long run, it is a very good investment in Xerox, in Xerox people, and in the community.

Recruitment. Xerox representatives state that some job applicants have cited the company's "social responsibility" as one reason they applied. This belief in the company's active social concern translates into what company publications term a recruitment "edge."

High Visibility. Although SSL is not a high profile program within Xerox, it has been featured in a number of articles in trade and popular press. Xerox has received almost 200 requests for information on the program's design and operation from other corporations. Some companies even have sent representatives to sit in on the employee evaluation selection process.

Participant Motivation. Many of the leavetakers have indicated their motivation is "to put something back into society." One employee who is blind, for example, worked with an agency providing service to the blind. Applicants do not view SSL as time to refresh themselves from job pressures, but rather as an opportunity to renew society's resources so that these services will be available for others when they need them.

Impact on Participants

Many leavetakers say that their social service has had a profound impact on their lives: they view themselves in a new perspective following their leave. Cahalan observes that this effect was most clearly demonstrated by changes in one of Xerox's salesmen. The employee's go-getter style of pursuing his goals resulted in a leading sales record, but he alienated co-workers by not considering their needs. He was granted SSL and he arrived enthusiastically with a concrete, detailed plan to improve the quality of life for an economically deprived group. Within a few months, his "I know best" approach to the implementation process had again alienated those working with him. However, the direct, honest, and open feedback he received helped him recognize that he needed to be sensitive to the needs of the clients to accomplish the project. And he learned that people want to have a say in the programs that affect their lives. Through the SSL experience, he developed a wide range of human relations skills which have benefited him personally and the company as well. His development of interpersonal skills enhanced his career development and contributed to his subsequent success as a Xerox manager.

SOCIAL SERVICE LEAVE

Wells Fargo & Company

Organizational Climate

During the 1970s, Wells Fargo* management formed a Corporate Social Responsibility Committee to coordinate ongoing community projects, develop new programs, and address emerging issues. The 1979 Annual Report states that companies "no longer are judged solely on the quality of their products and services, or the profits they generate for shareholders. Increasingly, business firms are being evaluated on how they relate to their employees, their customers, the communities they serve and to society as a whole." Wells Fargo has been involved in numerous community development programs, including loans to low and moderate income neighborhoods, reinvestment loans, student and consumer loan programs, and short term loans to nonprofit organizations experiencing temporary cash flow problems. The company was presented with the national Human Relations Award of the American Jewish Committee for exemplary community service; Wells Fargo itself presents an annual social service award to a deserving employee.

In what the company has termed "one of the most innovative of its ongoing programs," Social Service Leave (SSL) encourages employees to become involved in the community by providing paid leaves of up to six months to employees meeting certain service requirements. Leave is to be used for volunteer work in agencies, schools, or organizations of the employee's choice. Established in 1976, Social Service Leave was designed to give employees an opportunity to help solve social problems that concern them personally. The impetus for developing SSL was an awareness of a similar program at Xerox Corporation. Wells Fargo was the first west coast organization to offer such an option to its employees.

---

*Demographic information is provided on p. 215, Wells Fargo Sabbatical case study.

Program

Employees who have worked three years at Wells Fargo and are in good standing may apply to the Corporate Responsibility Department for one to six months of fully paid leave. During their leave, employees receive all fringe benefits and continue to accrue vacation leave. Further, salary reviews and increases are given on schedule, and seniority is not affected. Employees are guaranteed a return to the same job or to one having a similar grade, responsibility, and opportunity.

Selection Process

Eligible employees interested in SSL submit written applications to a subcommittee of four officers from the Corporate Social Responsibility Committee. They do not have to notify their managers of their intention to apply. Supervisors cannot prevent employees from taking Social Service Leave. However, if there is a critical need, employees may be asked to postpone the leave for a short period until adequate coverage can be worked out. Applications are accepted throughout the year.

Once the Committee favorably reviews an application, members meet with the employee in an informal interview to discuss the project further.

Criteria for Selection

The application asks employees to provide an outline and timetable of their projects and project goals, to evaluate the value of the project to the community, and to describe how their skills can effectuate the project's completion (see Exhibit A). In addition, the applicant must submit a letter of acceptance from the sponsoring organization.

According to Nancy Thompson, Administrative Assistant to the Corporate Social Responsibility Committee, the committee uses three criteria for selection:

- A well-defined, carefully considered project that addresses a specific social goal.
- A project that has a "multiplier effect," that is, one that will continue to benefit the community long after the person has returned to Wells Fargo (for example, forming a new chapter

WELLS FARGO & COMPANY
Social Service Leave
Application Form

Name_____

Department, A.U. Number and City _____

Telephone Extension _____

Name of Supervisor and Title_____

Number of Years Full Employment at Wells Fargo _____

1. What do you want to do and for which organization? *(Include the general purpose of the organization, the work you will be doing and your goals.)*

2. Explain the value you feel your work will have for the organization and the community.

3. What motivates you to do this work? *(Include your prior involvement with the organization and the reasons you became initially involved.)*

4. Describe the skills you will need for the project. Are your skills and experience compatible with the skills needed? How?

5. Will your efforts on behalf of the organization result in continuing benefits to it, after you leave? In what way? *(For example, will your work have enrolled new volunteers, established procedures or projects which will help make the organization more successful in the future or in some other way produce results which will be of continuing value to the organization after your social leave is completed?)*

6. How long of a leave are you requesting? For which month(s)?

7. Provide an approximate timetable of how you plan to accomplish your goal(s). (Include the amount of time by weeks or months that you expect to spend on each phase of your work.)

8. Attach a letter of acceptance from the sponsoring organization.

Return application to: Corporate Responsibility Department
14th Floor, Annex
A.U. No. 881

Refer questions to extension 4280 San Francisco, Corporate Responsibility Administrative Assistant.

of an organization, steamlining procedures, or training new volunteers).

- A creditable nonprofit organization with which the employee associates.

Participation

Between 1976 and 1980, 14 employees—5 men and 9 women—participated in the SSL program; most had served in a volunteer capacity with their selected organizations prior to the leave. Wells Fargo annually sets aside an aggregate of 24 months that can be divided among applicants for SSL. 1978 was the first year in which all 24 months of aggregate leave was utilized, with four employees taking 6-month leaves. Only a few applications which moved beyond the preliminary screening level have been denied.

Thompson emphasizes that SSL is open to all employees, not just to top executives. She observes that the salaries of participating employees generally have not exceeded $18,000. Among the participants have been an operation officer, a training representative, a computer programmer, a clerk, and a technical writer. About one-fifth of employees who have taken SSL have had more than 10 years of service.

Employees on SSL have worked in a variety of community organizations, involving themselves in a wide range of activities. One employee, a cancer patient herself, set up a new branch of the American Cancer Society. The mother of a physically handicapped child worked at a school for the physically handicapped. Other program participants have prepared a crisis intervention guide for volunteers at a suicide center, brought together young criminal offenders with prisoners at San Quentin so they could learn firsthand about the harsh realities of prison, and made presentations to corporations to obtain donations to meet specific needs of a woman's center serving women in Los Angeles' "skid row."

Applications are solicited through staff bulletins and articles highlighting projects in the company's employee magazine, *The Wells Fargo Banker.*

Impact

One SSL participant describes the program as "the ultimate perk." Several others describe their experience with superlatives such as "great" and "fantastic."

Many found that, because of the less structured and organized nature of the nonprofit organizations in which they were involved, they were in positions with greater responsibility and independence than their regular jobs permitted. They were able to transfer their business analytical skills to streamline operating procedures at many of the nonprofit organizations. Reentry into their less autonomous positions at the company after a lengthy absence has caused some adjustment difficulties. Another problem results from the employees' being out of the mainstream of the company's business and having lost touch with their jobs and co-workers. To ease the transition of returning to the more structured environment of Wells Fargo, the company arranges a meeting midway through the Social Service Leave for participants, their supervisors, and a personnel representative.

For many Wells Fargo employees, the paid leave provides a unique opportunity to spend a substantial amount of time involved in beneficial community projects. Participants say that adapting their business skills to nonprofit groups has sharpened their skills and heightened their confidence.

For the company, the program is a visible reminder of the type of community-oriented approach to which it is committed, and the community has responded with acceptance and praise.

SOCIAL SERVICE LEAVE

Control Data Corporation

Control Data Corporation (CDC)* offers two types of social service leave—short term and long term. Short term leave, which is unpaid, may be authorized up to 5 days each calendar year if work scheduling permits, to allow employees to participate in social projects (e.g., serve as scout leader at a summer camp).

Long term social service leave, which may range from one month to a year, may be paid or unpaid. Paid leave permits employees to work with nonprofit social service organizations while continuing to receive full pay, full benefits, and have guaranteed right of reentry at the same job or one of comparable pay and status. Exempt and nonexempt employees with a minimum of two years continuous full-time employment are eligible.

Application for long term social service leave can be made at any time. Employees must provide information on:

- Goals of the organization with which they propose to work;
- Description of what they will do;
- The specific results they hope to achieve;
- Special skills to qualify them.

Appropriate supervisors review the applications and submit them, with their recommendations, to the Social Responsibility and Concerns Committee. This committee then reviews the application and makes recommendations to the General Manager of Public Affairs, who is responsible for the final approval or denial of all requests.

If granted a long term social service leave, an employee is on temporary assignment and is transferred to the payroll of the Public Affairs Department. While on the assignment, the employee's liaison to CDC is the Manager for Community Relations, who provides administrative support as needed.

---

*Demographic information is provided in chapter 2, CDC part-time case study.

The position of an employee on long-leave assignment normally is filled by another CDC employee who has been cross-trained for the job or by someone recruited from the outside, usually hired on a temporary basis.

Social service leave was established in 1977. Ten employees participated on a long term paid basis through 1980. Among their projects have been creation of a nonprofit agency for the purpose of alleviating a disease, establishment of a career placement service at a local college, and establishment of a medical clinic in a Mexican village.

Until 1980, it was the employee's responsibility to take in initiative, that is, choose and make arrangements for an appropriate project. Recently, CDC began to post social service leave opportunities brought to the company's attention, further encouraging its employees to participate in community activities.

PHASED RETIREMENT

Varian Associates

Varian Associates is a high-technology research and manufacturing firm based in Palo Alto, California, with 27 plants in seven states and nine countries. Products include electron tubes and solid state devices, instruments for quality control, scientific equipment used to search for alternative energy sources and to analyze food, water, and waste products for harmful substances, and medical products such as radiation therapeutic equipment and diagnostic ultrasonic scanners. In 1980, the company's sales exceeded $600 million. This growth resulted in 1,000 new jobs, increasing employment to almost 14,000.

Program

The firm offers a reduced workweek option at proportionately reduced salaries to workers who are at least 60 years old, have five years of service, and are within 2 years of planned retirement. Eligible employees may decrease their schedules to four days the first year and three days the second; other variations—with a minimum 20-hour workweek—are acceptable. The limit for participation in the program is two years. Benefits available to full-time employees are offered to participants, but many are reduced in proportion to the hours worked or salary earned.

The transition retirement policy was developed in 1977 by top management following employee requests for graduated reductions in work schedules prior to retirement. As outlined in the company guidelines, the objective of the program is "to broaden employment alternatives available to employees and to provide interested employees a gradual transition from full employment to the usual reduced activity of retirement." According to Benefits Administrator Jim Harvey, the company has tried to maintain its early philosophy that "employees are associates," despite its rapid and substantial growth.

In 1977, management had "no idea" how much interest there would be in the reduced workweek, but it proposed initiation of the program and recommended ongoing evaluation to determine the flexibility of accommodating employee requests, the effectiveness of eligibility requirements and other program elements, and the need for revisions. The 1977 program guidelines note there may be special situations in which two half-time employees will fill one job (job sharing); however, such an arrangement has not yet materialized.

Participation

The number of participants ranges from 5 to 10 percent of eligible workers. Between 1977 and 1980, 15 to 20 employees, including 3 women, took advantage of the program. Participants represent all organization levels—skilled trade workers, assemblers, clerical workers, technicians, senior engineers, a senior scientist, and two directors of corporate departments.

According to Harvey, those who participated would probably have taken early retirement without the program. While participants generally have enrolled in order to increase leisure time while remaining active in their fields, some employees have gone on the program in order to build up a nest egg or to achieve a goal such as sending children to college or paying off a mortgage before retiring completely. Varian has no mandatory retirement age in the U.S.

Fewer females than male employees apply to the program, and a number of factors may account for the former's low participation rate. Many married female employees in the 58- to 62-year age span choose early retirement so that their withdrawal from the labor force will coincide with that of their older husbands. The lower number of women may simply reflect the fact that fewer of the company's employees are female (38 percent).

Administration

The company maintains that the program works best for functionally independent positions. Since most employees are involved in individualized work, most participants retain their positions. However, if scheduling changes cannot be worked out in the department, job reassignments may be required.

Program guidelines suggest that supervisors may have to move to nonsupervisory positions when entering the program, but such a step is not always necessary. For example, a department head who directly supervised 7 employees and managed a department of 150 workers assumed a reduced workweek schedule with only a minor change in responsibilities.

The company's flexible retirement program is discussed at both benefit and preretirement seminars and in company publications. Interested employees apply to their supervisors approximately three months prior to the requested participation date, since it might take several months to find replacements and suitable alternative jobs for applicants (see Exhibit A for employee's application form). The supervisors, in coordination with their own supervisors, determine if a suitable job assignment is available and a suitable job classification indicated, and whether a replacement is needed. An appropriate schedule is then drawn up. Supervisors submit a program review form (Exhibit B) to the personnel department, and final approval is granted by production division managers. An appeals procedure is available if the employee's request is denied, but there have been no such denials to date.

Policy guidelines address issues such as merit increases (participants remain eligible), overtime compensation (not anticipated, but premium rates are not paid until employees work in excess of 8 hours a day or 40 hours a week), holidays (paid when they fall on scheduled work days), and reversibility (if economic hardship ensues, return to full-time employment is possible).

Fringe Benefits

Program participants are eligible for the same benefits as full-time employees. Medical and dental benefits are retained in full, while sick leave and vacation time are calculated in proportion to the number of hours worked. Benefits tied to earnings, such as life insurance, long and short term disability insurance, and employer contributions to the retirement plan, are prorated.

The retirement plan, maintained by the company for all employees, regardless of position, involves company matching and profit sharing. The company matches employee contributions and adds 5 percent of before-tax earnings. Although reduced income during the 2 years preceding retirement can decrease the amount available for retirement income, employees in-

Exhibit A

APPLICATION FOR RETIREMENT TRANSITION PROGRAM

_____
                                    Date

TO: _____
     (Employee's Supervisor)

FROM: _____
       (Name of Employee)

I would like to be considered for participation in the Retirement Transition Program. I have at least five years regular service with Varian and (please check and complete _one_ of the following:)

☐ Attained age 60 on   _____
                                          (Date)

☐ Will be age 60 on   _____
                                          (Date)

I plan to retire on _____ and understand I will remain in the program until that time unless my personal circumstances would require that I request a change or the company's situation requires a change. I further understand that my salary and fringe benefit participation will be based on the reduced work week.

I would like to request the following work schedule and specific position or general type of work _____

_____

_____

_____

_____

_____

_____
Employee's Signature   Badge No.   Department No.

RETIREMENT TRANSITION PROGRAM REVIEW FORM

NAME OF EMPLOYEE
_____

REQUESTED STARTING DATE   ACTUAL STARTING DATE
_____

1. This application can be accommodated under the provisions of the Retirement Transition Program.

   The employee will be assigned job classification:

   _____   _____
          Number   Title

   ☐ which can be   ☐ will require changes to
      used without   conform to the duties
      modification   which have been
                                    attached.

   The employee will work the following schedule_____
   _____
   _____
   _____

   Additional manpower ☐ will ☐ will not be required when this employee begins working a reduced work week.

2. This application cannot be considered for the following reasons:____
   _____
   _____

3. Remarks: _____
   _____
   _____
   _____

_____   _____
Employee's Supervisor   Date   Personnel   Date

_____   _____
Supervisor's Supervisor Date   Product Div. Mgr.   Date

2020-00-07 7/77   Please Attach Application for Retirement Transition Program (1620-00-01)

terested in transition retirement can build up their retirement accounts by making voluntary contributions before entering or while participating in the program.

Future of the Program

Interest in the program declined in the first half of 1980; Harvey attributes the chan ge, in part, to the fact that inflation induces workers to remain at full salary. In addition, the company's elimination of any mandatory retirement age has caused some employees to consider extending their worklives. Another disincentive is the social security earnings test. Employees indicate they would consider the Retirement Transition Program more actively between age 62 and 65 if the test were modified.

Overall, company management belives the program meets the needs and desires of some employees, and it will continue to offer reduced workweek options.

PHASED RETIREMENT

RegO

Founded in 1908, RegO of Chicago, Illinois manufactures valves, regulators, and welding torches. Its workforce of 700 is predominantly male and mostly involved in production work. The production operation is machining and assembly.

Decisionmaking

The company philosophy, as expressed in RegO literature, is "respecting the individuality of each and every employee."

In 1974, RegO initiated a preretirement package offering special benefits to employees who had reached age 64. The program was set up prior to passage of the Age Discrimination in Employment Amendments (ADEA) of 1978: expected retirement age at that time was age 65. The intent of the program was to acknowledge the contributions of the company's older employees and to help those workers prepare for retirement. Personnel Manager Tom McGrath indicated that, even with discussion of retirement in company preretirement seminars, older workers generally were unprepared for a new lifestyle.

Program

When employees reach age 64, they receive literature describing the company's preretirement program. Designated Forum LXIV, the program provides all workers aged 64 extra time off during their final year. Eligible employees are entitled to one 3-day paid weekend during the third quarter of the year and to one paid week off during the last quarter, in addition to normal vacation and leave time. Eligible workers, called Senators by the company, have completely flexible working hours during the year and do not have to clock in.

In addition, RegO holds special ceremonies for the "Senators" and provides such benefits as one year's free lunches at the company cafeteria and two free physical examinations.

Participation

Between 30 and 40 employees have participated in the program, which is voluntary. Some employees do not want the attention and wish to work their last year as they have other years. Supervisors have and do continue to participate.

Program Changes

With passage of the ADEA, retirement at age 65 was no longer predictable and RegO adapted its policy to accommodate workers staying on past age 65. It published a notice to all employees advising them of the modification. If employees wish to stay past 65, they can participate in Forum LXIV one year prior to planned retirement. There are no penalties if an employee decides not to retire after participating in the program, but the benefits are a one-time-only option.

As part of the Forum program, RegO makes special provision for the selection and training of replacements for their soon-to-retire employees in management positions and technical and skilled jobs. For example, a replacement is selected for a management employee during the first quarter of the Forum program. Training is completed by the end of the second quarter. At the start of the third quarter, the "Senator" moves to a job that is "tailor-made to the 'Senator's' interests and skills" for the final two quarters of the Forum. There may be some complications should the "Senator" decide to stay on past planned retirement, but there have been none to date.

PHASED RETIREMENT

Connecticut Mutual Life Insurance Company

Connecticut Mutual Life Insurance Company was founded in 1846 and is the oldest life insurance company in Connecticut. Connecticut Mutual employs approximately 1,500 people. Of these, 1,111 are clerical workers. The workforce is predominantly female (67 percent), and of the total workforce, approximately 350 employees are over 50 years of age.

Program

A fully paid, extended preretirement leave program has been available to full-time employees at the company for "as long as anyone remembers," says James T. Carroll, Administrator of Employee Relations. Company policy offers leave of absence, with salary, during the two-year period immediately preceding retirement.

The length of leave is tied to service requirements. Full-time employees with 10 to 14 years of service are entitled to 22 days (the average work month), those with 15 to 19 years service to 33 days, and those with 20 or more years service to 44 days. If leave is not taken in the blocks of time designated by the company, it is forfeited. For example, preretirement leaves of 22 days must be taken at one time. Employees eligible for 44 days may not take less than 22 days in the year prior to retirement. However, no preretirement leave may be taken in the final six months of employment.

Policy guidelines note that "retirement from work activities, combined with separation from friends and established relationships, is often more of an adjustment than expected." The program, started at least 25 years ago, was designed to ease this work-to-retirement transition.

Initially, there were no restrictions on how and when the preretirement leave could be taken. Employees generally accumulated their leave and used it to retire ahead of schedule. This practice was inconsistent with the original company intent of assisting its employees to adjust gradually to retirement. Consequently, in 1978, the company revised the policy to require at least some leave be taken in a block and no leave to be taken six months prior to retirement. The following guidelines apply:

- Preretirement leave of 44 days may not be taken in periods of less than 22 days at a time and at least 22 days must be taken in the year prior to the retirement year.
- Preretirement leave of 33 days must be taken in two periods of 17 days and 16 days or in two periods of 22 days and 11 days. The longer period must be taken in the year prior to the year of retirement.
- Preretirement leave of 22 days must be taken at one time.

The program was started not on the basis of cost considerations but as part of a company policy to provide good benefits. While the company has collected data on the cost of paid leave time, this is not a prime concern of the program. "The policy continues to reflect a company attitude that we care for our people," Carroll states.

Among benefits offered are an employer-contribution pension plan that continues to credit years of service past age 65 for retirement benefits. Pension benefit levels are calculated on the basis of the highest five years of earnings. The company pays for hospitalization of its retirees and permits continued use of its medical facilities. It also offers merit days to full-time nonexempt employees who have less than 25 years of service and maintain good absence or lateness records. Eligible workers are credited with a half-day of leave for each of 10 designated time periods (e.g., January 1 to February 6), with some accumulation and carry-over permitted. A flexitime program has been in effect since 1975.

Administration

Although preretirement leave is tied to service years, employees are automatically notified by the company's benefits administrator about their retirement status and availability of retirement information when they reach ages 53, 58, 63, and 64. The notification letter includes a reminder of the preretirement leave, and the program is discussed at greater length at twice-yearly preretirement seminars.

Requests for leave are made to department heads and are coordinated with the Benefits Department. Supervisors work with employees on how and when leave will be taken, provided guideline requirements are met. Any employees who had indicated their intention to retire before the new policy went into effect were permitted to schedule time off under the old rules. Often, supervisors will train other workers to assume the duties of program participants while they are on extended leave. In only one instance was it necessary to work out a unique leave scheduling arrangement: a maintenance engineer who worked a 12-hour shift alternated weeks of work with weeks of leave.

Essentially, all employees meeting eligibility requirements take leave. About 20 employees a year become eligible. The State of Connecticut has eliminated mandatory retirement, but most employees at the company continue to retire at age 65 or earlier. Employees are eligible to retire as early as age 55.

Future Considerations

Management still is concerned that the program is not entirely meeting the company's objective of having employees structure a large amount of time and would prefer employees to take a significant amount of their leave at one time in the year before retirement. "We are faced occasionally with the problem of employees taking too little leave rather than too much," Carroll observes. "Employees take time off as vacation rather than as a time to assess how retirement may affect them. The preretirement leave program is here to stay. Through preretirement seminars we will encourage employees to use the leave for the purpose for which it was conceived—a transitional step—a testing of the waters toward the new career of retirement."

PHASED RETIREMENT

Tennant Company

Established in 1870, Tennant Company is a nonunionized manufacturing firm with operations centered in Minneapolis, Minnesota. In addition to two plants in Minneapolis and a nation-wide sales and service force, it has manufacturing and marketing facilities in Europe and North America, with a joint venture in Japan. Its workforce of 1,400 is approximately 70 percent male.

Decisionmaking

The request of a 61-year-old industrial engineer for a shorter workyear led to consideration and, ultimately, adoption by top management of a new policy for preretirement leave. The employee suggested to Industrial Engineering Manager John Davis and Vice President of Manufacturing Douglas Hoelscher that he work 9 months out of 12 for each of the three years preceding his planned retirement at age 65. Both Hoelscher and Davis sought approval from Kenneth M. Hall (then Personnel Director) who supported the request but cautioned that leave be granted only after the company had specified the conditions under which such a request might be granted any employee.

In a memorandum to President George Pennock, Hall—who now is Vice President of Personnel Resources—suggested policy guidelines for management-approved, unpaid leave rang-ing from one to three months for all Tennant employees aged 60 or over.

Hall believed the plan would help workers prepare for retire-ment and recommended adoption of the leave policy to the Management Committee. This committee—comprised of Ten-nant's president and top officers—met in 1975 and approved the recommendations.

Conditions for participation in the Preretirement Leave pro-gram are as follow:

- Any employee aged 60 or over who has one year of service may request a leave of absence;

- Leave is unpaid;
- Leave may be taken for no less than one month and no more than three months;
- Leave may be combined with part or all of normal vacation (unlike policies for other types of leave which require that earned vacation be used before leave begins);
- Leave must be approved by the department manager, Vice President of Personnel Resources, and the appropriate senior executive; and
- Participating employees may reapply for leave in subsequent years, subject to the same conditions.

Management philosophy is reflected in several of these provisions. For instance, workers with only one year of service are permitted to participate because, as Hall notes, "the problems employees face in retirement are the same whether they worked for Tennant or some other company." Likewise, the decision to offer unpaid, rather than paid leave was based, in part, on management's belief that workers should have a chance to learn about adjustment to reduced incomes and reduced work schedules. Cost consideration also influenced the decision.

When approving the plan, management was confident that jobs held by employees on preretirement leave could be covered for periods up to three months; in the past, staffing needs had been met adequately when workers were out for extended illnesses and vacations. Designated managerial personnel can disapprove a request if they think the reduced work schedule will interfere with operational efficiency. They also may suggest a shorter leave period, perhaps of one month rather than three, or a year's postponement.

Hence, leave is worked out on an individual basis. For example, a senior vice president requested reduced worktime. However, he foresaw problems in his taking three months of full-time leave, so he worked half-time between May and September instead. While phasing his retirement, he has begun to delegate responsibilities to subordinates.

Communication

When the program started, a feature article describing the policy appeared in Tennant's "Topics," the monthly employee newsletter. Now employees are informed of the program regularly in several ways. It is announced at the preretirement counseling seminars Tennant has offered since 1975 to employees aged 57 and over. It also is mentioned in the policy procedures covering a wide range of benefits, including retirement benefits, and is detailed in the personnel manual. Hall indicates that publicity of Prereitrement Leave is not a regular thing but refined communications are being planned to make employees more aware of this and other benefits.

Participation

The policy is "widely known among older employees," according to Hall. An average of 12 employees become eligible each year (personnel records show that from 1980 to 1986, between 7 and 19 workers will become eligible). Yet, of those eligible, approximately 6 employees have used the Preretirement Leave. Hall notes that these employees have enjoyed the leave and it has worked out well for the company, but the number is less than expected. He conjectures that, with an inflationary economy, workers can't afford to take unpaid time off. While Tennant continues to offer all fringe benefits except sick leave to employees on leave, the reduced salary has a negative impact on worker retirement benefits.

Given Tennant's profit-sharing plan, reduction in pay means a reduction in an employee's profit. To illustrate, a worker earning $24,000 annually may receive up to $3,600 in profit sharing as the profit share can be as high as 15 percent of earnings. (The profit share has been 15 percent in 7 of the last 10 years, and has averaged between 13 percent and 14 percent during that 10-year period.) If that worker took three months off, the annual salary would be $18,000 and the profit could be reduced by as much as $900 to $2,700.

Hall has suggested that, were the company to start a pension plan, leave time would probably be considered as paid time for the purpose of computing pension benefits. Hence, benefits for a worker earning $18,000 with the 3-month unpaid leave would be calculated on the basis of the $24,000 annual salary.

PHASED RETIREMENT

International Harvester Company

The International Harvester Company (IH) was formed in 1902 by the merger of the McCormack Harvesting Machine Company with four other farm equipment manufacturers. It later entered the automotive and construction equipment fields. With sales of $8.4 billion in 1979, IH now is a major manufacturer of agricultural equipment, gasoline and diesel powered trucks and tractors, construction and industrial equipment, and turbo-machinery. IH employs 98,000 workers worldwide, with approximately 60 percent of its workforce in 17 factories and 20 regional offices in the United States. Its headquarters office is in Chicago, adjacent to the site of the first factory Cyrus H. McCormack, inventor of the revolutionary reaper, erected in Chicago.

Nine of every ten IH workers are union members. The United Automobile Workers (UAW), which represents 35 percent of all company workers, is the largest union. UAW "sets the standard" for contract negotiations between the company and the more than 20 craft and trade unions affected.

Decisionmaking

In 1973, in response to UAW demands, the company developed a preretirement leave plan which provided partially compensated leave time for employees with 30 years of continuous service. The length of leave was based on an employee's age and extended from one to four weeks; workers could not receive cash payments in lieu of time off. (The plan is described in detail later.)

The UAW viewed the program as consonant with its commitment to job creation through worktime reduction and early retirement; a generous early retirement plan had been adopted during earlier bargaining sessions, and increases had been negotiated in subsequent sessions. (Effective October 1979, workers with 30 years of continuous service or aged 60 with 10 years service, were eligible to receive unreduced retirement benefits of about $800 per month, increasing to $950 a month by the end of the new agreement.)

By the 1980 contract negotiations, the local unions, which handled implementation of the preretirement leave program, felt the program wasn't meeting union objectives: the incremental increases in weeks off discouraged workers from choosing early retirement. By combining vacation and preretirement leave, employees could look forward to almost two months off when they were 56 years old. Local union leaders wanted the plan redesigned to provide an incentive for early retirement.

IH management similarly was interested in restructuring the preretirement leave program, primarily to reduce administrative and scheduling problems. Through the years, the UAW had bargained for a generous package of paid time off, including additional holidays and vacation days, Christmas holiday shutdown, and optional leave. The preretirement program created additional difficulties in planning for full utilization of facilities and equipment.

The new preretirement leave program now provides employees with 30 years of service a one-time option to take 15 weeks of leave, a lump sum payment, or a combination of time off and payments.

1973 Preretirement Plan

The 1973 plan, initially limited to hourly workers and later extended to nonmanagerial, nonunionized, salaried employees, provided eligible employees who had 30 or more years of continuous company service the option of electing time off with leave benefits. Leave ranged from one week for employees under age 52 to four weeks for those 56 and over, in increments as follow:

Age of employees as of January 1	Number of weeks of leave
Under 52	1
52	2
53	2
54	3
55	3
56 and over	4

Employees were notified of their eligibility prior to January 1. Leave was forfeited if not scheduled by February 1. Other conditions included:

- Employees had to have performed some work for company during the year they took the leave;
- Leave had to be taken in full workweek increments but not necessarily all at one time;
- No cash payments were given in lieu of leave time;
- Scheduling was arranged on the same basis as vacation, with employees consulting with supervisors. Supervisors attempted to accommodate individual preferences for time off, but also took into account production needs and vacation policies at the particular site;
- The rate of pay was equivalent to that received under the company's disability plan (approximately 65 percent of the employees' weekly wage).

During the first year, 69 percent of eligible employees used the extra time. Participation increased to almost 80 percent in succeeding years. The increase most likely resulted from favorable comments on the program by participants.

1980 Preretirement Plan

The 1980 UAW and International Harvester contract agreement substantially modified the earlier preretirement plan. Employees with 30 or more years of service are entitled to 15 consecutive weeks of preretirement leave. Thirteen weeks are paid at the weekly disability rate, and two are fully paid vacation weeks.

This is a one-time only benefit, to be taken immediately preceding retirement. Eligible employees may take less than 13 weeks of preretirement leave and receive pay in lieu of the time off for the unused portion. They may also elect to receive a lump sum payment for all the leave at retirement.

The contract sets out policies for dealing with vacation plans and holidays falling during preretirement leave (see Exhibit A).

The UAW estimates that 2,000 to 3,000 IH employees (average age 55) will be eligible for the preretirement leave over the two years remaining on the current contract. UAW's Education and Training Director Art Shy hopes that the changes in the length of leave and the lump sum payment option will serve as an incentive to early retirement. Even if workers don't retire early, he believes the length of the leave might create more employment opportunities.

Exhibit A

**International Harvester
and
International Union,
United Automobile, Aerospace
and Agricultural Implement Workers
of America**

May 2, 1980

Preretirement Leave   Article V

(d) In the event any holiday falls during the thirteen (13) weeks of Preretirement Leave Benefits, the Employe shall be ineligible for holiday pay. In the event any holiday falls in the vacation period immediately following the thirteen (13) weeks of Preretirement Leave Benefits, the Employe shall be entitled to holiday pay in addition to vacation pay as provided under Section (8)(e) of Article XIV of the Production and Maintenance Main Labor Contract and the corresponding provisions of the C&T and PDC&RW Labor Contracts.

(e) In the event an employe's thirteen (13) weeks of Preretirement Leave Benefits encompass a scheduled Plant vacation period, any vacation which would normally be allocated to the scheduled vacation period shall be paid in accordance with Section 6 of Article XV of the P&M Main Labor Contract and the corresponding provisions of the C&T and PDC&RW Labor Contracts. The Preretirement Leave will not be extended by such vacation payment. If an Employe receives vacation pay which otherwise would have been allocated to the scheduled vacation period, the Employe will be eligible for holiday pay for the Independence Day holiday which falls within the scheduled vacation period.

PHASED RETIREMENT

Mutual of Omaha

Mutual of Omaha was established in 1909. Headquartered in Omaha, Nebraska, the company sells and services health insurance and, through its principal affiliate, United of Omaha, life insurance. Approximately 65 percent of its Home Office workforce of 5,500 are female. Omaha is the center of a metropolitan area of more than a half million people. The region is the country's fourth largest insurance center. Additionally, it is a major communications center for such services as hotel reservations and credit card processing. It has a strong agriculture base; meat packing, though in somewhat of a decline, remains a large industry in the area.

Nebraska and the Omaha region have been relatively immune to recession and have one of the lower unemployment rates in the nation. Mutual of Omaha now is in keen competition with other firms for the declining number of high school graduates.

Program

In 1960, Mutual of Omaha established what the company refers to as a preretirement program for the purpose of training replacements for soon-to-be-retired employees. Another important objective has been to ease the adjustment into retirement for senior employees.

Mutual of Omaha provides extended paid vacation to employees aged 62 to 64 who have 15 years of service. The length of leave is tied to age:

62 years - 8 weeks
63 years - 10 weeks
64 years - 12 weeks

The program, set up prior to passage of the Age Discrimination in Employment Act (ADEA) Amendments, which extends mandatory retirement age to 70, was structured on the premise that employees would move into full retirement at age 65. At age 65, the employee can use the 12 weeks extended leave to retire three months earlier than the retirement date. Employees cannot take cash in lieu of the extended vacation time; nor can they store up extended leave and apply it to another year.

The company's intent was that employees would take vacations in large blocks of time to prepare for retirement. This is not happening, according to John R. Dixon, Vice President and Director of Personnel and Employee Services, who says that the vast majority of program participants prefer using their vacation time piecemeal over the course of the year. The one exception is that many employees, when they reach age 64, accumulate leave and use it to retire early.

The company has resisted imposing a condition that the leave be taken in blocks of time because that would contradict management philosophy regarding regular vacation. Traditionally, vacation is taken in a form convenient to the employee and compatible with work group needs. Requiring leave to be taken in blocks of time would be a major departure from past practices, Dixon notes, and a requirement employees would not be happy with.

The program was structured to coincide with a requirement of mandatory retirement at age 65—a requirement changed by the ADEA. However, passage of the ADEA has not had a great impact on the program. Mutual's experience has been that few employees continue to work beyond age 65.

Appendix

DESCRIPTION OF THE SHARED WORK UNEMPLOYMENT COMPENSATION PROGRAM

The Shared Work Unemployment Compensation (SWUC) program was established in California in 1978 as a supplement to the existing Unemployment Insurance (UI) program. Generally, the SWUC program was designed to work within the framework of the existing UI program. This appendix provides a brief description of the UI program along with a more detailed description of the SWUC program.

Overview of the Basic Unemployment Insurance Program

The Unemployment Insurance program involves both the state and federal governments. Generally, unemployment insurance taxes ("contributions") levied and collected by the *state* finance the payment of unemployment insurance benefits to eligible workers, while the tax levied by the *federal government* finances the administration of the unemployment insurance program at both the state and federal levels plus certain special unemployment insurance benefits. The federal tax rate currently equals 3.4 percent of taxable wages, as defined,[1] but federal law allows California employers a tax credit equal to 2.7 percent of taxable wages as long as California's unemployment insurance laws and regulations are in compliance with federal laws and regulations. Thus, the effective federal tax rate currently equals 0.7 percent of taxable wages. These taxes are collected by the federal government along with federal income taxes.

UI benefits are financed by employer contributions, and are paid by the Employment Development Department

---

1. Currently, taxable wages are equal to the first $6,000 of wages paid per employee.

(EDD) in accordance with federal and state regulations. EDD has the responsibility of setting each employer's UI tax rate, collecting the tax from the employer and making benefit payments to eligible claimants. The system keeps track of both the taxes paid by each employer and the benefit payments made to his/her former employees.

Centralized operations such as tax determination and data collection for the State of California are performed in the Sacramento office. Field offices located in over 150 cities across the state provide assistance to both employers and employees. These field offices verify claimant eligibility for UI benefits and compute benefit amounts.

The federal Department of Labor (DOL) has oversight responsibilities for the UI program. It reviews the administrative and benefit payment budgets of each state, and verifies state compliance with federal UI regulations. DOL also performs periodic audits of claims paid and administrative costs financed by the federal government.

The SWUC Program

Chapter 397, Statutes of 1978 (SB 1471, Greene), established the Shared Work Unemployment Compensation (SWUC) program in California on a temporary basis. It was enacted in the anticipation that Proposition 13, which had just been approved by the voters, would cause temporary disruptions in both the public and private labor markets. The original legislation called for the SWUC program to terminate on December 31, 1979. However, Chapter 506, Statutes of 1979 (SB 210, Greene), extended the program until December 31, 1981.

The purpose of shared work unemployment compensation, or short-time compensation as it is sometimes called, is to share the available work among employees during periods when reduced workload might otherwise lead to layoffs. To at least partially compensate employees for working reduced work hours, the program allows them, under certain conditions, to receive unemployment benefits for the portion of their normal workweek that has been curtailed.

Both employers and employees can gain or lose under the program. The employer must weigh the cost (in terms of higher UI tax payments) of the added unemployment insurance benefits received by employees against the savings resulting from not having to go through a "layoff-rehire-retraining" process when business picks up. In the case of the affected workers, those employees who would not have been laid off in the absence of the SWUC program must sacrifice a percentage of their regular earnings in order for those employees who would have been completely laid off to continue working.

An illustration of how this program works is as follows. Assume that a firm with 100 employees experiences a 20 percent workload reduction. The employer has two alternatives. One is to lay off 20 percent of the workforce; the other is to reduce everyone's workweek by one day (or 20 percent). Under the SWUC program the employees on the shortened workweek can collect unemployment insurance benefits for the one day per week that they are out of work. In this example, most employees would maintain about 90 percent of their regular take-home pay. In addition, they may continue to receive full health benefits as well as some or all of their regular sick leave, vacation, and retirement benefits.

The requirements that must be fulfilled in order for either an employer or an employee to participate in the SWUC program are outlined below.

Employer Eligibility Requirements

Workers facing a cutback in their hours can participate in the SWUC program only if the employer chooses to participate. In order to register for the program, the employer must submit to the Employment Development Department (EDD) a work sharing plan, which must be approved by the director of EDD. To be approved, the plan must satisfy the following requirements:

1. The reduction in wages paid and hours worked must be at least 10 percent in the affected work unit or units. Work units are defined by the employer.
2. If there is a collective bargaining agreement in effect, the bargaining agent must agree to the plan in writing.
3. The plan must identify all employees participating in the program and the reductions in each one's total wages and hours worked.

Anytime that there is a change in either the magnitude of the work reduction or individual workers covered by the plan, the employer must submit to EDD an amendment to the original plan.

The plans must also identify (1) the number of employees who would have been laid off if the SWUC program had not been available, (2) the reason for the work reduction, and (3) the number of expected weeks of reduced work. These considerations, however, do not have an impact on whether or not a work sharing plan will be approved.

Employee Eligibility Requirements

For an employee to qualify for SWUC benefits, he or she must be eligible for basic unemployment insurance (UI) benefits. In addition, the employee, or claimant, must have his or her total wages and normal workweek hours, as defined by the employer, reduced by at least 10 percent during each claiming period (a claiming period is equal to one week). If work hours are reduced by 100 percent during a claiming period, the employees are eligible for regular UI benefits, *not* SWUC benefits.

After a one-week noncompensable waiting period, a claimant may collect SWUC benefits for up to 20 weeks (claiming periods) during the 52-week period beginning with the week of the first payment. Under the SWUC program, a claimant does not have to show evidence of job search to remain eligible, as he or she would under the regular UI program, unless the employer has verified that the work reduction is permanent. If the employer offers increased hours of work, a claimant must accept the offer or be disqualified for benefits during that claiming period.

In order to verify that he or she has fulfilled these requirements, a claimant must submit a certification form for each week benefits are claimed. These certification forms are issued by the employer and submitted to the local EDD field office.

Employees such as seasonal, part-time, and intermittent workers, who traditionally have collected partial benefits, are eligible to receive SWUC benefits. If they collect SWUC benefits, however, they are not eligible for partial unemployment benefits. In almost all cases, a claimant will receive a larger award under the SWUC program.

If at any time an employee in the SWUC program is laid off, he or she becomes eligible for regular unemployment insurance benefits. However, the total of all benefits collected in any 52-week claiming period cannot exceed (1) 26 times the weekly UI benefit amount or (2) one-half of total base period earnings, whichever is less.

Employee Benefits

The benefits a claimant may receive under the SWUC program are based upon the amount he or she is eligible for under the regular UI program. The weekly benefit amount a claimant is entitled to is determined by the largest amount of wages received for any quarter during the claimant's base period. The weekly benefit amount is then reduced to reflect the percentage of wages received by the claimant, as shown in the work sharing plan submitted by the employer to EDD.

For example, if the largest amount of quarterly wages received by a claimant during his base period was $4,000, he would be eligible to receive $117 per week under the regular UI program. If his work sharing plan provided for a 20 percent reduction in work hours and wages, he would be eligible for $24 per week ($117 x 20% = $23.40). (Under current law, SWUC benefits are always rounded to the next highest dollar, and percentage reductions are figured to the nearest 10 percent.)

UI Contribution Rates

Current law requires that all "experience rated" employers make contributions to the Unemployment Fund. The term "experience rated" refers to the method by which an employer's UI contribution rate is determined. The employer's contribution rate has two components: (1) a *balancing account* contribution, and (2) a *reserve account* contribution. Both are assessed against the amount of each employee's taxable wages (currently, wages up to $6,000) according to certain factors.

The *balancing account* contribution rate varies from 0.1 percent to 1.0 percent of the employees' taxable wages, depending upon the ratio of balancing account charges to credits over the 24-month period ending June 30. The balancing account contributions are used to finance the payment of benefits in cases where the benefits cannot be charged to an individual employer's *reserve account.*

The *reserve account* contribution rate varies from 0 to 3.9 percent of the employees' taxable wages, depending on (1) the experience rating of the employer and (2) the ratio of the Unemployment Fund balance to total taxable wages statewide. Each employer's reserve account contributions are accounted for separately to facilitate computation of the contribution rate. These contributions are used to finance benefit payments to the employer's former employees. The ratio of the employer's reserve balance (contributions less benefit charges) to the employer's taxable payroll for the last three years is known as the experience rating. This experience rating determines the employer's tax rate. Two contribution rate schedules are used under the UI program. One, known as the high schedule, is effective any time the ratio of the Unemployment Fund balance is less than 2.5 percent of taxable wages statewide. The second, or low schedule, is otherwise in effect.

SWUC Contribution Rates

Certain employers are subject to an additional SWUC contribution rate. Employers who must pay this additional tax rate are those that meet the following criteria:

(1) The employer had a negative reserve account balance on the prior June 30, *and*
(2) The employer's reserve account had been charged with the payment of SWUC benefits during the 12-month period ending on the prior June 30.

In determining whether the second criteria has been met, the Employment Development Department (EDD) looks only for benefit charges from claimants identified on *that employer's* work sharing plan, although just as in the regular UI program, benefit payments are charged against the reserve accounts of *each* of the recipient's base period employers. Therefore, if an employer participating in the SWUC program has a former employee who is currently listed on another employer's work sharing plan, then SWUC benefits paid to that employee cannot trigger the imposition of the SWUC tax on the former employer. This insures that only the employers who are actually using or have used the program get charged with the tax.

SWUC Tax Rate Computation

For those employers who must pay the SWUC tax, the SWUC contribution rate is based on the employer's experience rating. The schedule of SWUC contribution rates is shown in Table A-1. The resulting contribution rates become effective each January along with the annual rates computed for the reserve and balancing accounts. These rates are applied to the taxable wages of the employer's *entire* workforce, not just the ones identified in the work sharing plan.

Table A-1
Schedule of SWUC Contribution Rates

Reserve Balance Ratio (Experience Rating)	Contribution Rate
-100% to No Limitation	3.0%
-80.0% to -100.0%	2.5%
-60.0% to -80.0%	2.0%
-40.0% to -60.0%	1.5%
-20.0% to -40.0%	1.0%
0.0% to -20.0%	0.5%

The first year in which SWUC contribution rates were levied was 1980. During the tax rate computation period for that year (July 1, 1978 to June 30, 1979) there were approximately 200 approved work sharing plans on file with EDD. Out of this group, 23 employers were assessed the additional SWUC tax, which generated approximately $3,400 in the first two quarters of 1980. Table A-2 shows how much revenue was collected from these employers.

Table A-2
SWUC Tax Rates and Revenue for 1980

Number of Employers	SWUC Tax Rate	Revenue[a]
17	0.5%	$2,503.33
4[b]	0.5%	- 0 -
1	1.0%	29.42
1	1.5%	867.69
Total 23		$3,400.17

SOURCE: Employment Development Department, Tax Control Bureau.

a. Revenue from first two quarters of 1980.

b. These employers did not generate revenue for various reasons.

The contribution rates for 1981 will not be determined until February 1981 (these rates are retroactive to January 1981). It is likely that the number of employers subject to the SWUC tax rate will increase in 1981. This is because during the computation period for determining the 1981 tax rate (July 1, 1979 to June 30, 1980), there were 1,022 approved work sharing plans, of which 92 represented employers with negative reserve balances.

Distribution of SWUC Tax Contributions

As discussed before, all revenue generated from any of the three unemployment taxes (reserve account tax, balancing account tax, and SWUC tax) goes to the Unemployment Fund, while all unemployment insurance and SWUC benefits are paid from this fund.

Current law requires that revenue generated by the SWUC tax rates be credited to the statewide balancing account, *not* to the individual employers' reserve accounts. On the other hand, SWUC benefits paid to claimants are accounted for in both the base period employer's reserve account *and* the balancing account if the employer has a negative reserve account.

Reimbursable Employers

Employers who elect reimbursable financing are not subject to the SWUC tax. As with the regular UI program, these employers must reimburse the Unemployment Fund on a dollar-per-dollar basis for their share of benefits paid out to current or former employees. Therefore, the very nature of this reimbursement method means that these employers cannot place an "undue burden" on the Unemployment Fund. Through September 1980, there were about a dozen approved work sharing plans from employers with reimbursable financing.

SCHEDULE OF BENEFIT AMOUNTS

Amount of wages in highest quarter	Regular UI weekly benefit amount	SWUC benefits for a 20% workweek reduction
$ 225.00 - $ 688.99	$30	$6
689.00 - 714.99	31	7
715.00 - 740.99	32	7
741.00 - 766.99	33	7
767.00 - 792.99	34	7
793.00 - 818.99	35	7
819.00 - 844.99	36	8
845.00 - 870.99	37	8
871.00 - 896.99	38	8
897.00 - 922.99	39	8
923.00 - 961.99	40	8
962.00 - 987.99	41	9
988.00 - 1,013.99	42	9
1,014.00 - 1,039.99	43	9
1,040.00 - 1,065.99	44	9
1,066.00 - 1,091.99	45	9
1,092.00 - 1,130.99	46	10
1,131.00 - 1,156.99	47	10
1,157.00 - 1,182.99	48	10
1,183.00 - 1,208.99	49	10
1,209.00 - 1,247.99	50	10
1,248.00 - 1,273.99	51	11
1,274.00 - 1,299.99	52	11
1,300.00 - 1,338.99	53	11
1,339.00 - 1,364.99	54	11
1,365.00 - 1,399.99	55	11
1,391.00 - 1,429.99	56	12
1,430.00 - 1,455.99	57	12
1,456.00 - 1,494.99	58	12
1,495.00 - 1,520.99	59	12
1,521.00 - 1,559.99	60	12
1,560.00 - 1,585.99	61	13
1,586.00 - 1,624.99	62	13
1,625.00 - 1,650.99	63	13
1,651.00 - 1,689.99	64	13

Schedule of Benefit Amounts (continued)

Amount of wages in highest quarter	Regular UI weekly benefit amount	SWUC benefits for a 20% workweek reduction
1,690.00 - 1,728.99	65	13
1,729.00 - 1,754.99	66	14
1,755.00 - 1,793.99	67	14
1,794.00 - 1,832.99	68	14
1,833.00 - 1,858.99	69	14
1,859.00 - 1,897.99	70	14
1,898.00 - 1,936.99	71	15
1,937.00 - 1,975.99	72	15
1,976.00 - 2,001.99	73	15
2,002.00 - 2,040.99	74	15
2,041.00 - 2,079.99	75	15
2,080.00 - 2,118.99	76	16
2,119.00 - 2,157.99	77	16
2,158.00 - 2,196.99	78	16
2,197.00 - 2,235.99	79	16
2,236.00 - 2,274.99	80	16
2,275.00 - 2,313.99	81	17
2,314.00 - 2,352.99	82	17
2,353.00 - 2,391.99	83	17
2,392.00 - 2,430.99	84	17
2,431.00 - 2,469.99	85	17
2,470.00 - 2,521.99	86	18
2,522.00 - 2,560.99	87	18
2,561.00 - 2,599.99	88	18
2,600.00 - 2,638.99	89	18
2,639.00 - 2,690.99	90	18
2,691.00 - 2,729.99	91	19
2,730.00 - 2,768.99	92	19
2,769.00 - 2,820.99	93	19
2,821.00 - 2,859.99	94	19
2,860.00 - 2,911.99	95	19
2,912.00 - 2,950.99	96	20
2,951.00 - 3,002.99	97	20
3,003.00 - 3,041.99	98	20

Schedule of Benefit Amounts (continued)

Amount of wages in highest quarter	Regular UI weekly benefit amount	SWUC benefits for a 20% workweek reduction
3,042.00 - 3,093.99	99	20
3,094.00 - 3,145.99	100	20
3,146.00 - 3,197.99	101	21
3,198.00 - 3,236.99	102	21
3,237.00 - 3,288.99	103	21
3,289.00 - 3,340.99	104	21
3,341.00 - 3,392.99	105	21
3,393.00 - 3,344.99	106	22
3,445.00 - 3,496.99	107	22
3,497.00 - 3,548.99	108	22
3,549.00 - 3,600.99	109	22
3,601.00 - 3,652.99	110	22
3,653.00 - 3,704.99	111	23
3,705.00 - 3,756.99	112	23
3,757.00 - 3,821.99	113	23
3,822.00 - 3,873.99	114	23
3,874.00 - 3,925.99	115	23
3,926.00 - 3,990.99	116	24
3,991.00 - 4,042.99	117	24
4,043.00 - 4,107.99	118	24
4,108.00 - 4,159.99	119	24
4,160.00 and over	120	24

SELECTED BIBLIOGRAPHY

Alternative Work Schedule Directory: First Edition, Washington, DC: National Council for Alternative Work Patterns, 1978.

A Review of the Shared Work Unemployment Compensation Program, Sacramento: Office of the Legislative Analyst, prepared by Betty Masuoka, January 1981.

Bednarzik, Robert W. "Worksharing in the U.S.: Its Prevalence and Duration," *Monthly Labor Review* Vol. 103, No. 7. July 1980.

Best, Fred. *Work Sharing: Issues, Policy Options and Prospects,* Kalamazoo, MI: W.E. Upjohn Institute for Employment Research, 1981.

Best, Fred. *Exchanging Earnings for Leisure: Findings of an Exploratory National Survey on Work Time Preferences,* Special Monograph, Office of Research and Development, Employment and Training Administration, Washington, DC: U.S. Department of Labor, 1980.

Best, Fred. *Flexible Life Scheduling: Breaking the Education-Work-Retirement Lockstep,* New York: Praeger Publishers, 1980.

Best, Fred and Gary Lefkowitz, Maureen McCarthy, Gail S. Rosenberg and Barry Stern. *Exploratory Survey on Short Time Compensation,* Unemployment Insurance Service, Office of Research, Legislation and Program Policy, U.S. Department of Labor, UI Occasional Papers Series, Forthcoming.

Best, Fred and James Mattesich. "Short-Time Compensation Systems in California and Europe," *Monthly Labor Review,* Vol. 103, No. 7, July 1980.

Bowers, Norman. "Probing the Issues of Unemployment Duration," *Monthly Labor Review,* Vol. 103, No. 7, July 1980.

Bradshaw, Ted K. *Cannery Workers Sabbatical Leaves: A Report on the Study of Thirteen Week Vacations,* Center for Labor Research and Education, Institute for Industrial Relations, Berkeley: University of California, 1976.

Butler, Robert. *Why Survive? Being Old in America,* New York: Harper & Row, 1973.

California Work Sharing UI Program: An Interim Evaluation Report, Sacramento, CA: Shared Work Evaluation Unit, California Employment Development Department (Fred Best, Project Director), April 1981.

Casey, Florence M. (ed). *Employment-Related Problems of Older Workers: A Research Strategy,* Research and Development Monograph 73, Office of Research and Development, Office of Policy Evaluation and Research, Washington, DC: U.S. Department of Labor.

Chapman, Brad L. and Robert Otteman. "Employees' Preferences for Various Compensation and Fringe Benefit Options," *The Personnel Administrator,* November 1975.

Clark, Robert L. *Adjusting Hours to Increase Jobs: An Analysis of the Options,* Washington, DC: National Commission for Employment Policy, Special Report No. 15, September 1977.

Cohen, Allan and Herman Gadon. *Alternative Work Schedules: Integrating Individual and Organizational Needs,* New York: Addison-Wesley Publishing Company, 1978.

Coming of Age: Toward a National Retirement Income Policy, Washington, DC: President's Commission on Pension Policy, February 1981.

Corbo, Jean M. "Part-Time Employment and the Elderly," Working Paper 1299-01. Washington, DC: The Urban Institute, September 1979.

"A Cure for Unemployment?" *Business Week,* October 29, 1979.

Davis, Louis E. "Alternative Organization Designs: In A Larger Perspective," Proceedings of the Alternative Work Patterns Conference, Atlanta: The American Institute of Industrial Engineers and co-sponsored by the National Council for Alternative Work Patterns, May 1980.

Deuterman, William V. and Scott C. Brown. "Voluntary Part-Time Workers: A Growing Part of the Labor Force," *Monthly Labor Review,* June 1978.

Fagan, J.W. "Work Sharing During a Depression," Speech, 1938.

Federal Employee Part-Time Career Employment Act of 1978, House Report No. 95-932, U.S. House of Representatives, 95th Congress, 2nd Session.

Freedman, Marcia. *Labor Markets: Segments and Shelters,* New York: Allanheld, Osmun, 1976.

Havighurst, Robert J. "Alternative Work Schedules: Implications for Older Workers," *The Journal of the College and University Personnel Association, 28,* No. 3, Summer 1977.

Hedges, Janice Neipert. "The Workweek in 1979: Fewer but Longer Work Days," *Monthly Labor Review,* Vol. 103, No. 8, August 1980.

Hedges, Janice Neipert and Geoffrey Moore. "Trends in Labor and Leisure," *Monthly Labor Review,* February 1971.

Henle, Peter. "Recent Growth of Paid Leisure for U.S. Workers," *Monthly Labor Review,* March 1962.

Henle, Peter. "Recent Trends in Retirement Benefits Related to Earnings," *Monthly Labor Review,* June 1972.

Henle, Peter. *Work Sharing as an Alternative to Layoffs,* Washington, DC: Congressional Research Service, Library of Congress, July 19, 1976.

Homjak, William W. "Layoff Rotation," *Personnel Administrator,* September 1978.

Jobs for the Hard to Employ: New Directions for Public-Private Partnership, Washington, DC: Committee for Economic Development, January 1978,

Jacobson, Beverly. *Young Programs For Older Workers: Case Studies in Progressive Personnel Policies,* New York: Van Nostrand Reinhold/Work in America Institute Series, 1980.

Kerachsky, Stuart, Walter Corson, and Walter Nicholson. *Shared-Work Compensation: A Research Agenda,* Prepared by Mathematica Policy Research, Inc. for the Office of Research and Development, Employment and Training Administration, Washington, DC: U.S. Department of Labor, February 1981.

Knatz, Hilary Fleming (ed). "Employment and Retirement: A Management-Labor Dialogue," *Proceedings of an Industry Conference on Employment and Retirement: A Pre-White House Conference on Employment and Retirement,* New York: Adelphi University Center on Aging, 1980.

Kreps, Juanita. *The Lifetime Allocation of Work and Income,* Durham, NC: Duke University Press, 1971.

Kreps, Juanita. "Some Time Dimensions of Manpower Policy," in Eli Ginzberg (ed), *Jobs for Americans* Englewood Cliffs, NJ: Prentice-Hall, 1975.

Leisure Sharing, Hearings of the Select Committee on Investment Priorities and Objectives, California State Senate, Sacramento, CA, November 1, 1977.

Levitan, Sar A. *Reducing Work Time as a Means to Combat Unemployment,* Kalamazoo, MI: W.E. Upjohn Institute for Employment Research, 1964.

Levitan, Sar A. and Richard S. Belous. *Shorter Hours, Shorter Weeks: Spreading the Work to Reduce Unemployment,* Baltimore: Johns Hopkins University Press, 1977.

Long, Marion C. and Susan W. Post. *State Alternative Work Schedule Manual,* Washington, DC: National Council for Alternative Work Patterns and National Governors' Association, 1981.

Lynton, Edith F. "Alternatives to Layoffs," Conference Report prepared for the New York City Commission on Human Rights, April 1975.

McConnell, Stephen R., Dorothy Fleisher, Carolyn E. Usher, and Barbara Hade Kaplan. *Alternative Work Options for Older Workers: A Feasibility Study,* The Ethel Percy Andrus Gerontology Center, University of Southern California, July 1980.

Meier, Elizabeth L. *Aging in America: Implications for Employment,* Report No. 7, Washington, DC: National Council for the Aging, 1977.

Meier, Elizabeth L. *Employment of Older Workers: Disincentives and Incentives,* Washington, DC: President's Commission on Working Papers, April 1980.

Meier, Gretl. *Job Sharing: A New Pattern for Quality of Work and Life* Kalamazoo, MI: W.E. Upjohn Institute for Employment Research, 1979.

Miller, Jeffery M. *Innovations in Working Patterns,* Washington, DC: U.S. Trade Union Seminar on Alternative Working Patterns in Europe, Communications Workers of America, May 1978.

Morand, Martin J. and Donald S. McPherson. "Union Leader Responses to California's Work Sharing Unemployment Insurance Program," Pennsylvania Center for the Study of Labor Relations, Indiana University of Pennsylvania: Working Paper Presented to First National Conference on Work Sharing Unemployment Insurance, San Francisco, May 1981.

Morrison, Malcolm. "International Developments in Retirement Flexibility," *Aging and Work,* Vol. 2, No. 4, Fall 1979.

Murray, Thomas J. "Work Sharing is Working in California," *Dun's Review,* August 1980.

Nealey, S.M. and J.G. Goodale. "Workers Preferences Among Time-Off Benefits and Pay," *Journal of Applied Psychology, 5,* No. 4, 1967.

Nollen, Stanley D. and Virginia H. Martin. *Alternative Work Schedules, Parts 2 and 3: Permanent Part-Time Employment and Compressed Workweeks,* New York: AMACOM, A Division of American Management Associations, 1978.

Nollen, Stanley D., Brenda Eddy, and Virginia H. Martin. *Permanent Part-Time Employment: The Manager's Perspective,* New York: Praeger Publishers, 1978.

O'Toole, James. *Work in America,* Cambridge, MA: MIT Press, 1974.

Owen, John D. *Working Hours,* Lexington, MA: Lexington Books, 1979.

Owen, John D. "Work Time: The Traditional Workweek and Its Alternatives," *Employment and Training Report of the President,* Washington, DC: U.S. Department of Labor, 1979.

"Paid Personal Holidays," *Solidarity,* October 21, 1977.

Platt, Robert. "Layoff, Recall and Work Sharing Procedures," *Monthly Labor Review,* December 1956.

Poor, Riva (ed). *4 Days, 40 Hours: Reporting a Revolution in Work and Leisure,* Cambridge, MA: Bursk and Poor Publishing, 1970.

(The) Productivity Problem: Alternatives for Action. Congressional Budget Office, Washington, DC: 1981.

Project JOIN: Final Report, State of Wisconsin: Division of Human Resource Services, Department of Employment Relations, Federal Manpower Programs Section, June 1979.

Quinn, Robert P. and Graham L. Staines. *The 1977 Quality of Employment Survey,* University of Michigan, Institute of Social Research, Conducted for the U.S. Department of Labor, December 1978.

Rehn, Gosta. *Prospective View on Patterns of Working Time,* Paris: Organisation for Economic Co-operation and Development, 1972.

Revisions of the Overtime Compensation Requirements of the Fair Labor Standards Act of 1938, Hearings before the Subcommittee of Labor Standards of the Committee on Education and Labor, U.S. House of Representatives, 96th Congress, 1st Session, October 23, 24, and 25, 1979.

Reynolds, Lloyd G. *Labor Economics and Labor Relations,* Englewood Cliffs, NJ: Prentice-Hall, 1970.

Rosenberg, Gail S. and Maureen E. McCarthy. "Flexible Retirement Programs in Two U.S. Companies," *Aging and Work,* Vol. 3, No. 3, Summer 1980.

Rosenberg, Robert. "A Pilot Project for Extended Leaves," Working Paper No. 10, Senate Office of Research, California State Senate, Sacramento, December 1976.

Rosenblum, Marc and Harold L. Sheppard. *Jobs for Older Workers in U.S. Industry: Possibilities and Prospects,* Washington, DC: American Institute for Research/Center on Work and Aging, September 1977.

Sheppard, Harold and Sara Rix. *The Graying of Working America,* New York: The Free Press, 1977.

Shkop, Yitzchak. *The Effect of Providing Various Options for Continued Employment in the Organization on Patterns of Retirement Plans,* Conducted under a grant from the National Commission on Employment Policy, U.S. Department of Labor, Forthcoming, 1981.

Singer, James W. "Sharing Layoffs and Jobless Benefits—A New Approach is Attracting Interest," *National Journal,* February 9, 1980.

Smith, Ralph (ed). *The Subtle Revolution,* Washington, DC: The Urban Institute, 1979.

Sugarman, Jule M. "The Decennial-Sabbatical Program," *Journal of College and University Personnel Association, 28,* No. 3, Summer 1977.

Swank, Constance. *Case Studies on Phased Retirement: The European Experience,* Washington, DC: National Council for Alternative Work Patterns, Forthcoming, October 1981.

Teriet, Bernhardt. "Gliding Out: The European Approach to Retirement", *Personnel Journal,* Vol. 57, No. 7, July 1978.

Teriet, Bernhardt. "Flexiyear Schedules—Only a Matter of Time," *Monthly Labor Review,* December 1977.

Unemployment Compensation Bills, Hearings before Subcommittee on Public Assistance and Unemployment Compensation of the Committee on Ways and Means, U.S. House of Representatives, 96th Congress, 2nd Session, Serial #96-113, June 26, 1980.

"Unions Campaign to Shrink Work Time," *Business Week,* April 24, 1978.

Wirtz, Willard and the National Manpower Institute. *The Boundless Resource,* Washington, DC: New Republic Book Company, 1975.

Work After 65: Options for the 80's, Hearings of the Special Committee on Aging, U.S. Senate, 96th Congress, 2nd Session, May 13, 1980.

"Work Sharing Programs Under UI," *California Public Employee Relations,* June 1979.

Work Time and Employment, Special Report No. 28, Washington, DC: National Commission for Employment Policy, October 1978.

Zalusky, John L. "Alternative Work Schedules: A Labor Perspective," *Journal of the College and University Personnel Association, 28,* No. 3, Summer 1977.

Zalusky, John L. "Shorter Hours—The Steady Gain," *AFL-CIO American Federationist,* January 1978.

Zalusky, John L. "Shorter Workyears—Earlier Retirement," *AFL-CIO American Federationist,* August 1977.

The National Council for Alternative Work Patterns, Inc. (1925 K Street, N.W., Suite 308, Washington, DC 20006) is a nonprofit research and resource group which provides information regarding flexible and reduced work hour schedules to management, labor, government, and special interest groups.